R. V. MISSIN
11 ALMA CHASE
TERRINGTON ST. CLEMENT

NIGHTMARE CONVOY

By the same authors:
Icekill
Hit The Beach
The Fate Of The Lady Emma
Night Of The U-Boats
Out Sweeps!
Trawlers Go To War
PQ17 — Convoy To Hell
The War Of The Landing Craft

NIGHTMARE CONVOY

The Story Of The Lost Wrens
By

Paul Lund & Harry Ludlam

W. FOULSHAM & CO. LTD.
London • New York • Toronto • Cape Town • Sydney

W. Foulsham & Company Limited
Yeovil Road, Slough, Berkshire, SLI 4JH

ISBN 0-572-01452-X

Copyright © 1987 Paul Lund and Harry Ludlam

All rights reserved.
The Copyright Act (1956) prohibits (subject to certain very limited exceptions) the making of copies of any copyright work or of a substantial part of such a work, including the making of copies by photocopying or similar process. Written permission to make a copy or copies must therefore normally be obtained from the publisher in advance. It is advisable also to consult the publisher if in any doubt as to the legality of any copying which is to be undertaken.

Printed in Great Britain at St Edmundsbury Press, Bury St Edmunds.

'And in the fourth watch of the night Jesus went unto them, walking on the sea.'

> St. Matthew, XIV.25
> Inscription on memorials to the lost Wrens

'Whenever I think of war I don't remember the happy things, but this convoy. It is my particular nightmare.'

> Nicholas Monsarrat
> Lieutenant in one of the naval escorts

Drawings by TOM SHUTTLEWORTH

Contents

    The Dark Days   9

1   The Flower of the Flock   11

2   Gibraltar Here We Come!   19

3   A Strange Goodbye   27

4   Night of Horror   37

5   More Wolves to the Kill   53

6   Flight from Slaughter   67

7   Missing, Presumed Drowned   81

8   Why Did It Happen?   95

9   Pennies for the Girls   103

10 A Life for Each Life   111

    The Memory   126

    The *Aguila* Wrens   127

    Acknowledgements   128

Illustrations

	Facing page
Sea Ranger Madge Barnes.	16
Chief Wren Madge on embarkation leave.	16
Happy band of Chief Wrens for Gibraltar.	17
Mrs Vera Laughton Mathews, Director, WRNS.	17
The Liverpool cruise steamer *Aguila* before the war.	32
Aguila after her gun duel with an enemy submarine.	33
Captain Arthur Frith, master of the *Aguila*.	48
Commodore's Yeoman of Signals Fred Buckingham.	48
L.A.M. William Churchouse, Fleet Air Arm.	48
The 'gift' destroyer USS *Hopewell*.	49
Hopewell when she became RNN *Bath*.	49
Corvette HMS *Campion*.	64
Corvette HMS *Wallflower*.	64
Coder Walter Wilkinson, HMS *Zinnia*.	65
Commander Charles Cuthbertson, RNR, captain of *Zinnia*, on whom the hero of *The Cruel Sea* was based.	65
Kapitanleutnant Adalbert Schnee, U-201.	65
Oberleutnant Reinhard Suhren, U-564.	65
Lieutenant-Commander Cuthbertson and his No. 1, Lieutenant Harold Chesterman, RNR.	80
Lieutenant Chesterman on Northern Patrol.	80
Nicholas Monsarrat: the convoy became his nightmare.	80
The rescuing ship's boat from HMS *Campion*.	81
Leading Seaman Geoff Drummond, leader of the rescuers.	
Telegraphist Tom Shuttleworth of HMS *Wallflower*, this book's artist.	81
Launching the lifeboat *Aguila Wren* at Aberystwyth.	96
Captain Cuthbertson and Walter Wilkinson now.	97
Zinnia rescuer Geoff Drummond.	97
Aguila survivor Fred Buckingham.	97
Aguila survivor William Churchouse.	97
Dedication of the *Aguila* Wrens memorial seat at Scarborough.	97

THE DARK DAYS

THERE is a cross standing without a grave in a churchyard in Aberystwyth; a small memorial plaque in the vestibule of St. Paul's parish church, Leith; and an old lifeboat of the Royal National Lifeboat Institution, retired after twenty years' service and used for training Sea Cadets at Scunthorpe, in Lincolnshire.

All are links with a wartime tragedy that still haunts the dreams of people today.

It happened in August 1941. At that time there was no such thing as 'World War II'. After two years of war with Germany and her Axis partner, Italy, Britain still fought on alone, aided by free forces which had fled the Nazi occupation of Europe. The USA remained neutral (Pearl Harbour was still three months away). And now Hitler had cynically torn up his non-aggression pact with Stalin and sent his armies scything into Russia.

In these dark and desperate days, the resources of the Royal Navy were stretched to the utmost in the Atlantic battle to secure Britain's lifeline of food and supplies, escorting convoys that sailed across the far ocean as well as those in waters nearer home. The capitulation of Vichy France had given the enemy prime bases on the doorstep for his marauding surface raiders, planes and U-boats to attack the British convoys. It was a battle that had gone increasingly in the enemy's favour.

In this month of August, the sailing of another convoy from Britain to Gibraltar was hardly of special importance in the grim and ever-widening conflict, though on a smaller canvas its need was vital.

When convoy OG71 set out from Liverpool on 13 August 1941, its leading merchant ship, the modest cargo and passenger steamer ss. *Aguila*, carried a large number of Service passengers including an excited company of young Wrens. The OG stood for the convoy's destination — 'Outward Gibraltar'. The Wrens, highly trained cypher officers and wireless telegraphist ratings, were the first ever draft to be sent to Gibraltar, where their skills were urgently needed. All the girls were eager volunteers for overseas service, and all of them had been carefully hand-picked by the Director of the Women's Royal Naval Service herself.

Apart from the unusual and very welcome presence of the pioneer band of Wrens, convoy OG71 was just another bold run to the Rock by an unremarkable assortment of cargo steamers escorted by a number of small naval warships. Or it might have been — until the enemy struck with devastating results.

Rumours of what had happened persisted afterwards in the Navy and the WRNS, but no report of the fateful convoy was given at the time nor any mention of it ever made public, even at the end of the war. Scant reference was made to it in official war histories; even in the official history of the WRNS it was apportioned only one short paragraph.

This is the full story of the tragic convoy OG71, told for the first time. It is written from secret wartime Admiralty documents, naval signals, Reports of Proceedings by escort commanders, merchant masters' and officers' reports, and the harrowing testimony of survivors then and now.

1
THE FLOWER OF THE FLOCK

1

THE FLOWER OF THE FLOCK

LITTLE Madge Barnes was a bundle of energy, a lively Edinburgh girl fairly brimming over with life. At sixteen, the oldest in her company of Girl Guides, she eventually proved such a high-spirited handful that her Guide leader asked the skipper of the local Sea Rangers if she would take Madge among her girls. The skipper agreed, and so Madge joined the company of Sea Ranger Ship *Persevere* at Leith.

It was just what she wanted. She had been longing to become a Sea Ranger, the branch of the Guides that followed naval drill and practised naval crafts — and actually messed about in boats. For a girl whose father and grandfather were both sailors, this was heaven.

From being the oldest of her Guide troop Madge now became the youngest in the nautical company, but she soon settled in and her progress was rapid. She had graduated in the Brownies for semaphore and in the Guides for morse, after tapping away for hours on a morse key at home with her older sister Anne, who was never fast enough for her. Now little Madge, of the vivid blue eyes in a round, merry face, plunged into her Sea Ranger activities with redoubled enthusiasm.

This was in the late summer of 1938, at the worrying time of the Munich Crisis. But the ugly threat of war seemed to have been lifted when Hitler finally talked peace with Britain, so nothing disturbed the girls of SRS *Persevere* as they went during the autumn holiday to stay at Blackness Castle, just on the edge of the Forth. This was the ultimate treat for Madge; she had only to see a ship in the river when she would rush out, stand on the highest rock she could find and semaphore to it.

During the following year of 1939 Madge, working as a shop girl in Edinburgh, continued her zestful life with the Sea Rangers. The girls used nautical terms for everything, wore Sea Ranger tally-bands, made out their own lanyards, and for drills had a bosun's pipe instead of a whistle.

Among their many activities they would go rowing on the canal at Redhall, but the expert eye of the girls' coach soon saw that Madge had little need of instruction for she proved to be a born seawoman. The company could not have had a finer coach than Captain James Smith. He was a famous merchant master who had made newspaper headlines around the world in the 1920s when, as first officer of the ss. *Trevessa*, which sank far out in the Indian Ocean, he steered an open ship's boat full of survivors to safety in Mauritius after a remarkable journey of 1,700 miles. His captain also saved the men in a second boat.

As late summer came round again, so the war clouds returned over Europe. Captain Smith admitted that this time things really looked bad. The week before Hitler marched on Poland, Madge had just one question: if it came to war, did he think it would go on long enough for her to join the WRNS? Captain Smith looked gravely at the intense faces of his patriotic young girls.

'I hope,' he said, 'it will not last that long — for all our sakes.'

Days later, on 3 September 1939, war was declared between Britain and Germany. Within a week Madge celebrated her seventeenth birthday and at once sent in her application to join the newly reformed WRNS. She was turned down, being under age. Disappointed but undaunted, she joined the local Civil Defence Volunteers and bided her time, all through the winter and spring of the 'phoney war', followed by defeat in Norway, the retreat from Dunkirk, the wholesale collapse of Europe under the Nazi jackboot and the threatened invasion of Britain.

One day early in September 1940, as the Battle of Britain raged in the skies, Madge excitedly phoned her Sea Ranger skipper, Winifred Shand, to tell her that she had posted off a new application to the WRNS the night before.

'When are you eighteen?' asked her skipper.

'This morning!' cried Madge delightedly.

She was accepted promptly and called up within a few weeks. Margaret Watmore Barnes, to give Madge her full name, had finally realised her dream. She packed her things for London.

She enjoyed her initial training at Greenwich, followed by a wireless course, and quickly showed such a flair for the work that, despite her young age, in only a few months she was made a Chief Wren Signals. The early summer of 1941 found her at Scarborough, on the Yorkshire east coast, which had become one of the bases for wireless telegraphist Wrens.

Already, the young girls in navy blue were a familiar part of wartime life in that town. The Hotel Cecil was their 'Wrenery', a comfortable billet in which most of the girls had their own 'cabins'. It was a high building looking over a park to the sea, and sometimes on a warm summer's day after a night watch at the shore wireless station, instead of going to bed girls would find a spot on the grassy bank leading down to the glen and read and doze for a few hours.

The wireless station was manned mostly by wireless officers from the Royal and Merchant navies. No young sailors here, most of the officers were father figures, and very kind they were; their wives would often invite the girls to tea.

The Wrens worked hard on a four-watch system; and sometimes, when staff was short, a three-watch system. Very tiring. But they were young enough to adapt to the odd sleeping times and played hard on off-duty days. There was never a lack of invitations to other Services' dances and parties, and many girls also hitch-hiked over the moors and dales, discovering the beauty of Yorkshire. Because of the watch system they would find themselves with different friends at different times and there was a great sense of comradeship. The girls came from all parts of the country. They did not talk much about their earlier lives; after all, these were dull by comparison, the 'now' was all absorbing. They were involved in a great adventure, helping to fight the war by doing a man's job, as close to being an effective part of the senior Service, the Royal Navy, as a woman could be.

And now there was the further adventure of service overseas, for under new arrangements Wrens could volunteer to go abroad as and when the opportunities arose. Already, two small companies of Wrens had left for Singapore. Now there was another posting coming up — the very first draft of Wrens to be sent to Gibraltar. Girls rushed to volunteer. Among them, naturally, Madge Barnes, the youngest Chief Wren of them all.

Every girl under the age of twenty-one had to obtain parental permission to volunteer for overseas. Mrs Lillias Barnes knew it was no good refusing Madge, although she was still only eighteen, for she had set her heart on it. She just had to be there!

The despatch of a company of her W/T Wrens to the key naval base of Gibraltar was an immensely important move for Mrs Vera Laughton Mathews, Director of the WRNS. The hard-pressed signals officer at Gibraltar had made urgent appeals to the Admiralty for skilled replacements. He had naturally expected men and was highly dismayed to be told that none were available but that he could have Wrens instead. The harassed officer only grudgingly accepted the Admiralty's offer when bluntly told it was that or nothing.

Mrs Laughton Mathews determined to surprise that officer out of his life. She had encountered this male reluctance, scepticism and even downright hostility all her life; she would counter it now, she vowed, by sending to Gibraltar her very, very best girls — the 'flower of the flock'.

In August 1941 the WRNS had not yet achieved its later immense proportions. It was still possible for the Director to know many junior officers personally and to select with the utmost care those required for specially important tasks. And this was vitally important: the first draft of Wrens to go to Gibraltar, the great battleship base, home of fighting Force H, where naval officers from sub-lieutenant to admiral were dubious if not acidly dismissive about the capabilities of Wrens for the responsible and very confidential work for which they were needed.

'Girls? What bloody use will they be!'

Mrs Laughton Mathews was a woman supremely equal to the challenge. She was by no means a figurehead of the WRNS — she *was* the WRNS. For she had rebuilt the Service, recreated it from nothing.

Nor did she meet the conventional idea of a female 'brasshat'. She was a big woman with a big heart, and with a young family of her own.

The daughter of a naval officer and historian, she was now in her early fifties, the mother of two young sons and a teenage daughter. And she drew on a life of rich experience, battle scarred from her efforts as an early campaigner for women's rights.

At the age of twenty, Vera had been caught up in the Women's Suffrage movement, flinging herself into it with all the fervour and enthusiasm of which she was capable, standing in the gutter selling copies of the *Suffragette* while male passers-by actually spat on her. On the outbreak of the Great War in 1914, when women's Services were still undreamed of, she had trekked up to the Admiralty to offer her services as a humble

Left: Sea Ranger Madge Barnes, early in 1940.

Right: Chief Wren Madge with her nephew on embarkation leave in 1941.

Above: Happy band of Chief Wrens bound for Gibraltar. Back row: Phyllis Bacon, Ellen Waters, Mildred Norman, Madge Barnes, Catherine Slaven, Nursing-Sister Kate Gribble (QARNNS), Mary Grant, Elsie Shepherd, Beatrix Smith. Front: Dorothy Bonsor, Rosalie Wells, Madeleine Cooper, Cecilly Benjamin.

Mrs Vera Laughton Mathews, Director of the WRNS. Her girls were all hand picked, "the flower of the flock."

Photo: Fleet Air Arm Museum

clerk, but there were no women civil-servants in the Admiralty in those days and she was firmly told, 'We don't want any petticoats here!' So off she went to work as a journalist, but when the formation of a volunteer Women's Royal Naval Service was announced just before Christmas in 1917 she rushed to join. And as the Wrens, against much opposition, gradually took over a variety of naval duties ashore, she became an officer in charge of one of the biggest units in the Service, winning out against male suspicion and the general belief that 'women are no good'.

The WRNS was abruptly disbanded at the end of that war, in 1919, after less than two years' existence, but such was the extraordinary spirit, dedication and comradeship of the fledgling force that in spite of its official demise it lived on in other ways; the Association of Wrens was formed, with a flood of membership. But this old comrades' association did not stop at socials and annual dinners, it affiliated to the Girl Guides Association and gave that movement active support. A nautical branch of the Guides was formed, eventually known as the Sea Rangers.

Throughout the inter-war years, as a tireless worker for women's organisations both in Britain and internationally, Vera Laughton Mathews also worked hard for these budding girl sailors. Guide Commissioner and chairman of all the London Sea Ranger companies, she was until 1939 skipper of one Sea Ranger crew herself, never happier than when taking her girls rowing, swimming, signalling, camping, or on a fortnight's exploration of the canals in a converted ship's pinnace with a canoe as tender — with her devoted husband along as head cook and bottle washer.

Vera's crew were all young London working girls, most of them shop assistants, absolute 'townies', but they became really skilled at handling boats, even though it entailed getting up at the crack of dawn for lessons on Regent's Park Lake, with the early morning mist lifting off the water, before their day's work began.

When, early in 1939, with the rumbles of war sounding ever more menacing, it was decided to restart the WRNS, Vera Laughton Mathews was a natural choice for appointment as its Director. She was given a back room at the Admiralty, left to get on with it, and once again had to face male indifference and hostility, having to fight for her Wrens all the way over quarters, rankings, everything, even when war came and with it a new urgency. Now, in 1941, her wholly volunteer force was becoming established, but as yet with less than a quarter of the strength it would later achieve (100,000 women served in the WRNS during the war). So it was still possible for this lady of great verve and great heart to know most of her girls. And she understood them all, of all ages, as she certainly understood the bouncing vitality of talented young Madge Barnes, a girl not much older than her own daughter, who would also join the Wrens when of age.

And so to the girls for Gibraltar. From eager volunteers the Director herself chose nine young Wren cypher officers; then, with two senior officers, she held a selection board for the Chief Wrens, from whom were chosen the lucky twelve to go, including the exuberant Madge. It was quite an excited 'family' atmosphere. There were two other Scots girls, from Inverness and Glasgow, while among those from the South was Mildred Norman, formerly a 'Nippy' waitress at a Lyons Corner House in London, who was one of the local Sea Rangers who had used to go along to Mrs Laughton Mathews' home in St. John's Wood for country dancing. A young naval nursing sister was selected to complete the party. Twenty-two girls in all.

In no time at all Madge and the rest of them were home on embarkation leave. Under long-standing and rigid Admiralty regulations, women were not allowed to travel in warships, so they would have to be found passage in an armed merchant passenger ship in convoy.

Before leaving Scarborough to join a convoy for Gibraltar the happy Chief Wrens and the nursing sister posed for an unofficial group photograph on the steps of their 'Wrenery', the Hotel Cecil. They wore full uniform including the school-girlish hats rudely referred to by naval officers as 'pudding basins', being little different from the old-fashioned headgear worn by the original Wrens in the Great War. Two of the girls could not be present when the photograph was taken so their hatless faces were superimposed on the picture later. And there it was, a complete record of the pioneer draft of Chief Wrens for Gibraltar (the officers would join the company from other bases): Ellen Waters, Catherine Slaven, Mary Grant, Beatrix Smith, Madge Barnes, Phyllis Bacon, Mildred Norman, Elsie Shepherd, Madeleine Cooper, Dorothy Bonsor, Rosalie Wells, Cecilly Benjamin, and Nursing Sister Kate Gribble of Queen Alexandra's Royal Naval Nursing Service.

Thirteen in all. But no one was superstitious. It did not seem ominous at the time, why should it?

2
GIBRALTAR HERE WE COME!

2

GIBRALTAR HERE WE COME!

THE convoy the Wrens would join was designated OG71, the 'OG' standing for Outward Gibraltar. But before that code name could be written with a flourish on confidential documents there was a lot of work to be done. Organising a convoy, any convoy, was never easy.

Once again it was the headache of trying to round up a number of suitable ships made ready for sailing and bring them together at the same starting point at a certain time. Secret cypher messages flew back and forth between the Admiralty in London, the Commander-in-Chief Western Approaches, and naval officers in charge at the various key ports.

Likely ships were earmarked for OG71 then despairingly cancelled; some were delayed by engine trouble and other defects, others just could not be ready and in the right port of departure at the right time. Even at the very last minute two vessels selected for the convoy had to be deleted from the list and another one substituted, hasty alterations that were not always shown on official documents. Matters were not helped by having to arrange the convoy's departure date to coincide exactly with the availability of warships to escort it, these being greatly overworked and having to go directly from one convoy to another much like trams halting at a terminus only for as long as it took them to turn round.

In the event, OG71's preferred sailing date had to be postponed to await the arrival of sufficient naval escorts, while another convoy had to be cancelled altogether to allow OG71 to go ahead.

Then suddenly time had run out and the weary naval controllers could only sit back and pray that each ship listed for OG71 would put to sea at the right time and without further snags.

The plan eventually arrived at was for the nucleus of the convoy, consisting of five ships including the Commodore ship, to sail from bomb-battered Liverpool and join up off Belfast with two other, larger groups of ships, one of these sailing up from Milford Haven and the other steaming out from the Clyde.

Then, the whole convoy assembled, OG71 would take the North Channel, sailing round the northern coast of Ireland, past Malin Head and the Bloody Foreland and well out to the west. At a certain point it would then turn southward, steaming roughly parallel to the west coast of neutral Eire; then on down to Gibraltar, executing a great curve to the west in order to keep it at a good distance from the coast of occupied France and the enemy's probing planes and his U-boats operating from Lorient.

Every convoy needed to have a Commodore ship. That is, an armed merchant vessel in which a senior naval officer — designated a Commodore of convoys — took quarters with his naval signalling staff and assumed overall control of the merchantmen, liaising with the senior commander of the naval escorts. The Commodore ship chosen for OG71 was the ss. *Aguila*, a Liverpool cargo and passsenger steamer which in peacetime had plied her trade with the Canary Islands.

The *Aguila* was owned by the shipping line of Yeoward Brothers, who had traded with the Canaries, Spain and Portugal since the 1890s; such was the Liverpool firm's popularity that their name was mentioned in a number of island folk songs. Yeowards used the Spanish colours of red, yellow and red for their house-flag, with the bold black letters YB on the yellow portion; and their small fleet of five ships were each given Spanish or Portuguese bird names, all beginning and ending with the letter 'a'. *Aguila* stood for eagle.

It seemed only yesterday that *Aguila* and her sister ships had been embarking on their popular sunshine voyages to Lisbon, Madeira and the Canaries, each taking some eighty passengers on a twenty-one-day cruise for £21 as they went on the round trip to pick up cargoes of tomatoes, bananas and potatoes. The Yeoward ships had been a familiar and distinctive pre-war sight on the Mersey, their three masts and funnel aft, a tradition carried over from the days of sail, making them easy to identify among other vessels on the river. A Yeoward ship could then be seen in dock any Saturday morning; one sailed for the Canaries every week. Now here was the *Aguila*, her proud house colours hidden under drab warpaint, loaded with general cargo for Gibraltar and preparing to embark not cruise passengers but a large number of Service personnel destined for Gibraltar and the Middle East.

Both Yeoward Brothers and *Aguila* herself had already had their brushes with the enemy. During the recent heavy air raids on Liverpool by German bombers the Yeoward headquarters in James Street had been totally destroyed, the firm having to continue as best they could from temporary premises. Much earlier, the *Aguila* had seen front-line action at sea.

Exactly a year ago, in August 1940, *Aguila* was sailing from Lisbon to Las Palmas when, 259 miles from land, Captain Arthur Frith, while studying his charts, heard an explosion and at once thought his ship had been torpedoed. As he rushed from the chart-room on to the bridge he heard another explosion, and on looking round saw that a submarine had surfaced on *Aguila's* starboard quarter less than three miles away. The shell from its first gunshot had missed the ship by only twenty feet.

Through the heat haze over a flat calm sea the menacing submarine with its large conning tower was all too clearly visible. Would it now try to torpedo them?

Captain Frith immediately manoeuvred to bring the enemy astern, sounded the klaxon for gun stations and the crew of the four-inch opened fire. The captain put *Aguila* at her best speed of fifteen knots and wherever the enemy shells fell he steered in the direction of the burst, so as to upset the calculations of the enemy gunnery officer as he tried to correct his aim. The submarine retaliated by putting itself beam on and increasing its fire with two guns. The action continued for a full fifty minutes, with the enemy turning first on one beam then the other, his shots alternately falling short then very close ahead.

Aguila's gunners got off twenty rounds, only half as many as the enemy, but their last half dozen shots fell uncomfortably close to the submarine which, just as Captain Frith was preparing to use his smoke floats as a screen surprisingly broke off the action. *Aguila* kept at her best speed and reached Las Palmas without a scratch.

The quick thinking of Captain Frith in this engagement was quite in character, for he knew his ship and he knew the waters, and he certainly did not know the meaning of surrender. Short in stature but lacking nothing in skill and guts, Frith had sailed the world before joining the Yeoward Brothers line. He had survived the 1914–18 war when the ship he was in struck a mine; in the 1930s he received an award from the Liverpool Shipwreck and Humane Society for taking *Aguila* to the rescue of the crew of a steamer abandoned in the Irish Sea. A strict disciplinarian but always fair, very fastidious, particularly in his appearance, always optimistic and with a good sense of humour, Captain Arthur Frith was popular with his crew and passengers alike, a master to respect and trust. He was now fifty-one years old and had spent a lifetime at sea.

As the Liverpool section of OG71 prepared to sail, Captain Frith was joined on *Aguila* by the convoy's Commodore and his staff.

Vice-Admiral Patrick Parker had come out of retirement at his home in Chertsey, Surrey, snugly called 'The Haven', to volunteer his services on the outbreak of war. Tall and slim, he was one of the old school of RN officers, gentlemanly in manner, quiet and dignified, more like the headmaster of a public school or a high Churchman than an admiral, so unlike the bluff and bullying types who were all too common.

Parker had entered HMS *Britannia* as a naval cadet back in 1895 and reached the rank of commander before fighting his first war against the Germans in 1914–18, winning the DSO as captain of a monitor in the Dover Patrol. After captaining cruisers he became assistant director of naval equipment, and before retiring in the early 1930s served a ceremony-filled year as naval ADC to King George V. Having retired early he was still only sixty years old, a very fit man, and now embarking on yet another convoy through waters which he knew almost as well as the master of *Aguila*.

Parker's naval staff of seven which he took with him in *Aguila* were led by Yeoman of Signals Fred Buckingham. For him, the forthcoming voyage would be a new milestone in his young life, for he had been married in Liverpool only a few days before. On *Aguila* he had charge of two wireless telegraphists and four signalmen who would keep a constant signals watch twenty-four hours a day for the duration of the convoy. As the

Commodore's right hand man, Buckingham himself would be on the bridge from dawn to dusk, plus any other time necessary.

Now all was ready, all the passengers on board. There was a total of eighty-four, all naval personnel, including members of the Fleet Air Arm and, of course, the unexpected and attractive company of twenty-two Wrens. The crew, including the master, the Commodore and his staff, and five naval gunners totalled seventy-seven, which gave *Aguila* a full complement of 161.

She was by far the largest ship in the Liverpool section of OG71, as her passengers discovered on running a curious eye over the rest of the small flock. Three were nondescript steamers, the *Spero*, *Ebro* and *Lapwing*, all barely half *Aguila's* 3,300 tons and carrying general stores for Gibraltar; but the fourth, the *Stork*, although even smaller, was a trim-looking motor vessel. Only Captain Frith and Commodore Parker knew from their convoy list that *Stork* was loaded to the hilt with jerrycans of petrol.

Wednesday 13 August 1941. Dawn. The part-convoy's two escorting warships had now arrived and sailing was imminent. The senior escort, the sloop HMS *Leith*, was a lean and fairly modern small warship of under 1,000 tons, having been built in the mid-1930s. She had returned from peacetime duties in the Pacific to fight the war and was already a veteran of many Atlantic convoys.

The big surprise was the second vessel, a very strange-looking warship with no fewer than four funnels. Although larger than *Leith*, the destroyer *Bath* was considerably older — and American. A survivor of the Great War, she was one of fifty 'over-age' destroyers which had been given to Britain by the USA in return for concessions in the West Indies. Formerly the USS *Hopewell* she had been in service with Group 5 of the Liverpool Escort Force for less than three months. She was manned by a captain, officers and men of the free Royal Norwegian Navy together with a handful of British naval men.

Just before OG71 raised anchor, *Leith's* commander passed to Commodore Parker an amended secret route for the convoy from the Commander-in-Chief, Western Approaches. This changed route would bring them closer in to the coasts of France and Spain as they made their way southwards, though still maintaining what was considered to be an adequately protective distance to seaward. Throughout the voyage the convoy was to make frequent changes of course, especially at night, following a zig-zag pattern to deceive enemy air and sea forces as to its position and final destination.

13 August: 2 p.m. Logged by HMS *Leith*: 'Sailed from Liverpool with Liverpool section of OG71 (*Aguila* and four others) and RNN *Bath*.'

On this beautifully warm and sunny afternoon many of *Aguila's* passengers were on deck to see their slow progression into the Irish Sea led by the two warships. Most had written letters home to be posted for them after they had sailed. All the Wrens had done so, like Madge Barnes, who had also written a special letter to her old skipper of the Sea Rangers at Leith, Winifred Shand, with whom she had kept in touch during her months in the Wrens. Madge wrote:

Dear Skipper,
By the time you get this I shall be well on my journey. I am leaving this letter along with one for my mother with the officer and she will post them when she thinks enough time has elapsed since our departure.

At the top, you will find the address of my new abode. If you send a letter by airmail (5d.) it will only take 12 days, whereas if you send one by sea it will take three weeks. It would be nice to find a letter waiting for me when I arrive.

If anything should happen to me, Skipper, I want you to know that the happiest moments of my life were when I was at a Sea Rangers muster. I liked the Guides very much, but somehow I liked being in the 'Seas' a lot better. I guess that this is because I am crazy on the sea, and it gave me my first connections with it.

Please write straightaway. Until I hear from you again –
I remain your 'Lone Sea',
MADGE

Ships' crews were waving to each other now, and especially to the happy party of Wrens on the deck of the Commodore ship, none more excited than little Madge Barnes, the smallest and youngest of their company. It was a happy coincidence for the ex-Sea Ranger from Leith that the senior warship leading the convoy should bear the name of her old crew's town.

In just three weeks' time she would be nineteen years old . . . and she would celebrate that birthday in Gibraltar!

3

A Strange Goodbye

3

A Strange Goodbye

THURSDAY 14 August. The Liverpool section of OG71, forging through a sunlit sea, was joined in the North Channel by ten ships which had sailed up from Milford Haven, having left that port a day earlier. All smaller than *Aguila*, most of the new arrivals were around the 2,000 tons mark or a little less, like their leader, the ss. *Ciscar* (1,809 tons) from London, which carried stores for Gibraltar.

Seven of the ten vessels were British. One, the ss. *Spind*, was Norwegian, while the other two were neutral Eire vessels, the ss. *Clonlara* and ss. *Lanarhone*, both from Limerick and both unarmed; but neutral ships of many flags now joined British convoys following Hitler's decree that neutral ships too could be sunk on sight without warning by his roaming U-boats. Like the majority of other vessels, the Irish ships were laden with coal for Lisbon via Gibraltar.

Early next morning — **Friday 15 August** — the third section of six ships from the Clyde joined the convoy. At first it seemed that only five vessels had made it, but the little ss. *Switzerland*, a humble British coalship despite her name, which had dallied behind, cracked on her best steam to catch up. One of the Clyde ships was Greek, carrying pitch in bulk, all the others were British, carrying stores or coal, like the ss. *Alva* from Glasgow, laden with more than 2,000 tons of it, though two vessels were in ballast including the ss. *Grelhead*, which at just over 4,000 tons was the biggest ship in the convoy.

There was one more arrival, the ocean-going steam tug *Empire Oak*, from Oban. She was only 482 tons but was piratically armed with a twelve-pounder and two Hotchkiss guns operated by three naval gunners, plus two parachute and cable (PAC) rockets. These were the rather doubtful inventions which, when fired against low-flying aircraft, zoomed up, dangling in their wake lengths of piano wire which hopefully entangled the enemy and put an end to his capers. Most of the merchant ships carried two of these rockets besides their emergency flares. The rest of their assorted armaments were much the same as on *Aguila*. A four-inch or twelve-pounder, a couple of Hotchkiss and two or more Lewis guns, whatever they had been able to 'scrounge'. One vessel boasted a pair of Gatling guns.

The ships carried a mixture of naval and merchant gunners. *Aguila* had five naval gunners, while *Ciscar* was fortunate enough to have nine; she had also managed to acquire no fewer than six Lewis guns and a Hispano as well.

So here they all were, the convoy was complete. Commodore Parker studied his convoy papers and checked off each vessel. There were twenty-two of them altogether, including *Aguila*. The *Ciscar* (Captain E.L. Hughes) was to act as Vice-Commodore ship.

For *Aguila's* passengers, as for all the convoy crews, a comforting sight was the arrival of the rest of OG71's naval escorts. With the Clyde section had come three Flower-class corvettes, HMS *Hydrangea*, HMS *Campanula* and HMS *Bluebell*. Now two more came, HMS *Campion* and HMS *Wallflower*. These new, small and chunky escort ships, all named after flowers of the English garden, were coming out of the shipyards as fast as they could be built to play an arduous part in the sea war. They had originally been intended as coastal escorts only, but the needs of the situation now committed them to work in deeper seas. Identical in appearance, constructed from a whale-catcher design, the corvettes were limited in speed and armament, their main weapons being a four-inch gun of 1918 vintage and a store of depth-charges, but they were good seaboats, if frequently alarming in performance. Like the type of fishing vessel from which they were spawned they did not cut through waves but rode over them, rolled, bobbed and weaved, sat on the tops of waves, spun round like corks and generally bounced about to the discomfort of their long-suffering crews, who swore that the lively vessels would roll on wet grass. The corvettes were heavily overcrowded and cramped for space, carrying far bigger crews than they had ever been intended to carry as coastal escorts; but at least no turbulent seas seemed likely on this summer voyage to the Rock.

The convoy laboriously formed up into columns and steamed off, Commodore Parker soon having his signalmen busy as he ordered the merchant ships to practise emergency turns. During the day they were joined by another corvette, HMS *Zinnia*, members of her crew, as she passed close to *Aguila*, delightedly waving and blowing kisses to the Wrens on deck. Six corvettes now, added to their leader, *Leith*, and the destroyer *Bath*; eight close escorts in all. As they steamed on their screening positions, ahead and on the flanks, they were a bold sight.

OG71 headed north-west round the northern-most tip of Ireland at a steady seven knots.

Saturday 16 August. Clear skies and continuing warm. Perfect weather. Some distant ships were glimpsed, then from overhead came a friendly 'buzz' by two Blenheim bombers and a patrolling Hudson of Coastal Command.

Frequently, on watch-keeping within the convoy, a head would turn to the deck of *Aguila*. Nice to have a bit of glamour around!

Sunday 17 August. Early morning, and a ship in trouble. The *Grelhead* reported to the Commodore that she was unable to keep up owing to incompetent firemen. The convoy's speed was reduced to six and a half knots. Stern signals from Commodore Parker followed. *Grelhead* finally got up steam and rejoined, giving no further trouble. The convoy settled down once again to a uniform seven knots.

10.35 a.m. A Wellington bomber appeared on the convoy's port bow. It was speedily identified by *Wallflower*, but . . . consternation. The old four-stacker *Bath* opened fire on the surprised plane, which hurriedly flew off. There followed an icy signal to the Norwegian destroyer from *Leith*. *Bath's* excuse was that the Wellington, when challenged by signal lamp, had given her the wrong reply.

11.20 a.m. Admiralty wireless signal to *Leith*: 'Long range enemy aircraft are operating in your vicinity. Attack may be expected.'

Almost immediately, right on cue it seemed, a shadowing aircraft appeared astern. It was quickly identified as a Focke-Wulf Condor, one of the enemy's big four-engined bombers which had been taking such a heavy toll of British ships in the Atlantic. The menacing plane circled, meeting with bursts of anti-aircraft fire from the nearest escorts, but did not attempt to select a target. Instead it withdrew well out of range and continued to shadow them for some time. Then suddenly it had gone, and shortly afterwards the probable reason was seen: another patrolling Hudson. Then, with a cheery signal, this plane too had flown off.

The convoy continued at an uninterrupted seven knots, course west-south-west. But the arrival of the Focke-Wulf shadower had caused concern to at least one thoughtful merchant master. By steering WSW — far out into the Atlantic — the convoy was carefully giving no indication of its ultimate destination, and yet the clues were there to see for anyone conversant with normal peacetime shipping movements in the North Atlantic.

Captain Hughes, on the bridge of the Vice-Commodore ship *Ciscar*, leading one of the columns of ships, looked across at *Aguila*, leading another column. The three-masted vessel was unmistakably one of the Yeoward Line, all that company's ships were so designed; and as the Canary cruisers also traded to the Spanish ports, could not the hostile aircraft have recognised her and reported accordingly? There were also the two Eire ships which, unlike the British, still sailed as neutrals in full house colours. They had very distinctive red and white funnel markings, immediately identifiable, and it would not have taken an expert to deduce from their presence alone that the convoy must be bound for Gibraltar.

Anxious eyes watched the sky during the afternoon but the shadower did not return.

10.30 p.m. A patrolling Catalina flew over the convoy. So warmly familiar, these big, American-built flying boats. A welcome visitor, presaging a quiet night?

At last, when they had seemed to be steaming so far westward that they would continue across the Atlantic to America, the course of the convoy was altered more to southward, beginning the great arc that would take them down past the west coast of Ireland and then the outer limits of the Bay of Biscay on their journey to the Rock.

The Liverpool steamer *Aguila*, popular for her Canary Islands cruises, shortly before the outbreak of war.

Aguila in wartime paint at Madeira in 1940 after her successful gun duel with an enemy submarine.

= ORIGINAL ROUTE
= AMENDED ROUTE

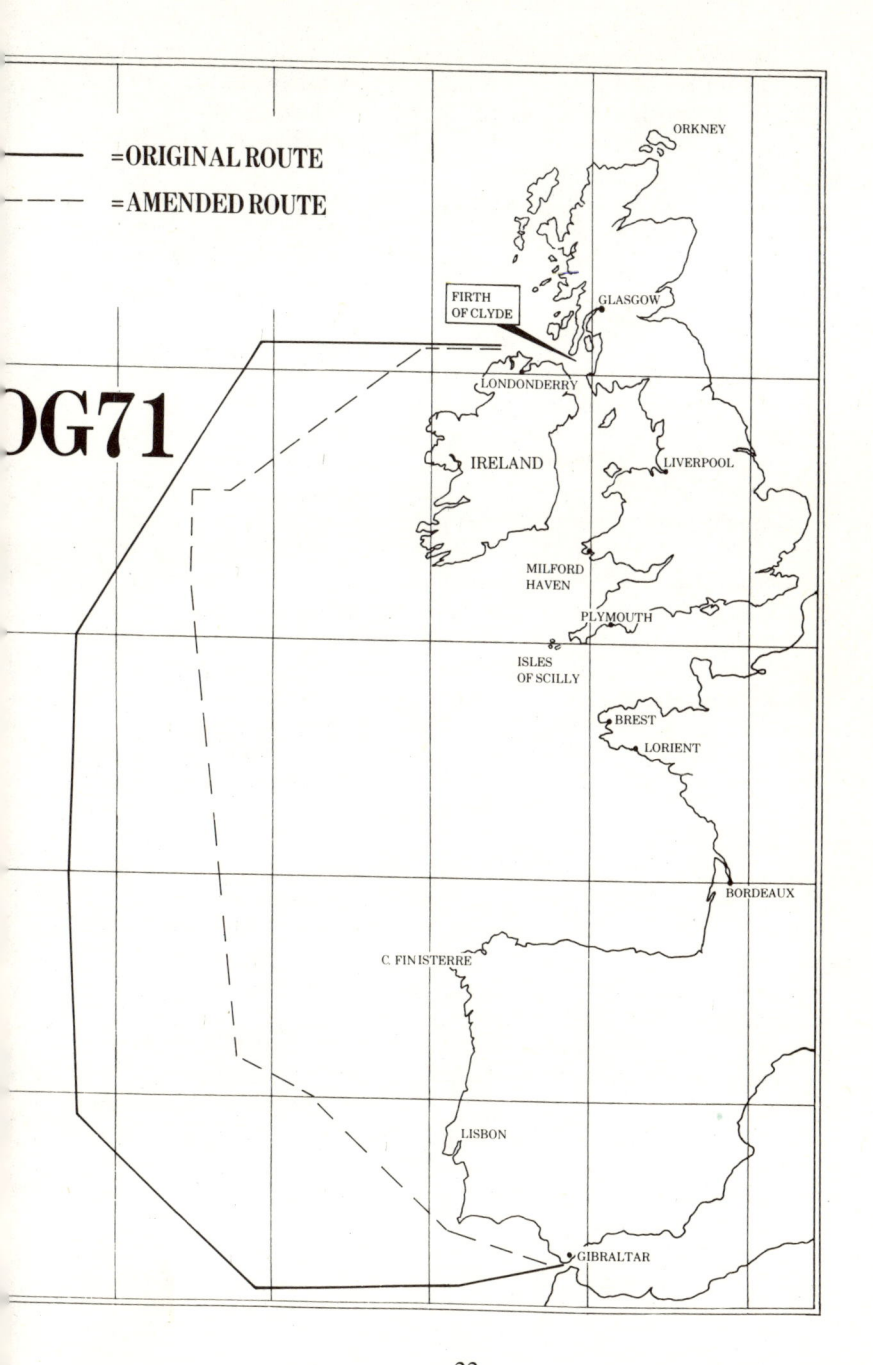

OG71

Monday 18 August. At 2.04 a.m. the peace of the early hours of the night was broken by a warning signal from Admiralty to *Leith*: 'More than one U-boat may be shadowing convoy.'

It was comforting that the circling Catalina remained with them till dawn before flying off.

It was another fine, warm day. The *Aguila* could well have been on one of her sunshine cruises instead of leading a wartime convoy. HMS *Leith* steamed ahead of the group of ships, with the corvettes deployed on their various screening positions like so many sheepdogs.

11.49 a.m. Admiralty to *Leith*: 'D/F (direction finding) bearings indicate three or four U-boats may be in your vicinity.'

A firm warning now of several underwater prowlers. But the afternoon remained quiet, except for one of the Eire ships lagging dangerously behind and having to be bullied along by a corvette. When danger did come it was again from the air.

In the early evening two Junkers 88 bombers flew over to circle the convoy at long range, then very suddenly swooped down out of a clouded sky. It was all so fast and, in a way, a great relief for the gun crews on board several ships — at last they had something definite to shoot at.

The German planes had chosen the plum target of the ss. *Grelhead*, the biggest ship in the convoy and, being in ballast, riding high in the water. A total of eight bombs whistled down on the *Grelhead* and her nearest neighbour, *Empire Stream*. Surprisingly all missed, though some fell very close, and a veritable flood of anti-aircraft fire followed the planes as they roared off. The range was not very good but both escorts and merchantmen resoundingly let fly. *Ciscar* showed her considerable sting with a stream of lead from her Hispano, Hotchkiss and Lewis guns, while *Aguila's* gunners also put up a brisk curtain of fire, unfortunately one of her foremast stays being damaged either by one of her own Lewis gunners or the overenthusiastic gun crew of another merchantman.

The action was over as suddenly as it had begun, the enemy planes speeding to extreme range and eventually over the horizon. The big question was: had they really gone, or were there others lurking out of sight? There was an uneasy feeling that the convoy was still being shadowed.

6.51 p.m. Admiralty signalled *Leith*: 'D/F bearings indicate that four or five U-boats are in the vicinity of convoy OG71.'

All the escorts were now keenly on the alert. As yet there had been no sign of any U-boat activity, but the Admiralty's warnings were based on superior RDF (radio-direction-finding) reports. Commodore Parker signalled all merchantmen: 'Submarines in the vicinity. No smoke or lights to be shown.' The first part of this order meant that ships should trim their boiler fires evenly so as to avoid making excess smoke, a certain give-away in the sky to a searching enemy.

Precautions were taken in another quarter. Minutes after the Admiralty's latest signal a message went out from C-in-C Western Approaches to HMS *Wanderer*, an escort destroyer operating farther to the west, giving the convoy's estimated position and instructing: 'Proceed OG71 and carry out sweep astern of convoy for two hours before returning. Convoy is being shadowed by U-boats.'

The old V and W destroyer from the last war steamed at once to carry out orders.

It was a fine evening turning to twilight with a moderate sea. Having left the west coast of Ireland behind, the convoy was now proceeding on its southerly course far to the west of the Bay of Biscay. On board *Aguila* spirits were high as her threshing engines took them on calm, untroubled course for the Rock.

'Put that cigarette out!'

The Commodore's yeoman, on his way back to the bridge in the gathering dusk, had spotted a Wren absent-mindedly smoking on deck. She sheepishly extinguished the tell-tale pinpoint of light.

With everything quiet, Captain Frith left the bridge to go down to dinner, stopping to talk to a steward in the top bar on the way. Just then a Wren officer passed by and the master sociably asked if she would like a drink. She was delighted to accept the captain's invitation, but he was disconcerted when, on finishing her glass, the girl stood up and held out her hand to him.

'I would just like to say goodbye,' she said, 'and to thank you and your crew for all the help you have given us.'

'Goodbye?' said the surprised master. 'What do you mean? I'll say goodbye to all of you when we reach Gib!'

'But this is goodbye for me,' replied the girl solemnly, 'and I wish you all the luck in the world, but you don't need my good wishes — you'll survive.'

Captain Frith smiled and gravely thanked her before going on his way. It was a strange thing for the Wren to have said but she was so earnest he did not wish to embarrass her by further protestation. He dismissed the incident and thought no more of it.

The high spirits of the passengers found an outlet that night. After dinner there was an impromptu concert in the saloon. One of the naval lads pounded through the old favourites on the piano and there was a lively sing-song. For the finale, Second Officer Christine Ogle lined up her whole company of Wrens, already proudly dressed in their Gibraltar whites, to sing 'The World Is Waiting For The Sunrise'.

It was a rousingly sentimental finish, a row of pretty girls singing the words with all the gaiety of youth. Mrs Laughton Mathews would have been well pleased with them. From little Madge, and ex-'Nippy' Millie Norman, to Phyllis Bacon, who sang with especial fervour knowing that her brother was serving elsewhere at sea in the battle-cruiser *Repulse*; and among the eight Third Officer Wrens, Margaret ('Peggy') Chappé Hall, only daughter of one of the original Chief Officers of the WRNS, and Cecilia Joy, the only Irish girl in the party, carrying on the tradition of her aunt who had been a senior officer in the WRNS in the last war and lost her sight on service.

For all of them it was a night for sentiment and unashamed patriotism; for high optimism, and fun.

Meanwhile, well to the rear of the convoy, HMS *Wanderer* had arrived and made her two-hour anti-submarine search as ordered, but found nothing. Just before midnight, *Leith* ordered destroyer *Bath* to drop back and make a fresh, exhaustive sweep closer in astern.

4
NIGHT OF HORROR

4

NIGHT OF HORROR

TUESDAY 19 August, 1 a.m. Kapitanleutnant Walter Kell, creeping up on the convoy in the surfaced U-204, sighted ahead in the darkness the unmistakable silhouette of the old four-funnelled destroyer *Bath*, zig-zagging at twelve knots on her sweep two and a half miles astern of the columns of merchant ships.

A quick confirmation, and Kell fired two torpedoes.

On board *Bath*, sharp-eyed lookouts glimpsed a low, dark object on the starboard beam which was quickly identified as an enemy submarine. A moment later, before illuminating starshell could be fired, a torpedo track was seen. *Bath's* captain, Lieutenant-Commander Fredrik Melsom, immediately ordered evasive steering but it was too late — in seconds the torpedo tore into the destroyer's engine-room, followed closely by another.

There was a vivid flash and a thunderous explosion as the disembowelled warship at once broke in two. Men were pitched or jumped desperately into the dark sea as she sank in a horrific three minutes, plunging to the bottom in waters 2,700 fathoms deep. As her stern section slid below the surface, two depth-charges set at a hundred feet exploded, killing many hapless men as they struggled in the water.

The corvette HMS *Hydrangea* saw the violent explosion from her position with the convoy three miles ahead. Her captain, Lieutenant Woolfenden, RNR, turned and steamed back at speed, *Hydrangea* trembling at the underwater blast of the depth-charges as she closed in.

Flares were spotted on the water in the darkness and men were heard shouting, but they could not be seen. *Hydrangea* lowered a boat to search for survivors. Badly wounded men were dying in the water, others struggling helplessly, their clothing and skin covered with oil fuel. The rescuers had been working for over an hour, pulling agonised men from the odiously strewn sea, when HMS *Wanderer* arrived and also lowered a boat to assist. The urgent work went on, listening for and following the foreign cries of the Norwegians, desperately searching in the dark — for unlike merchant seamen, the naval men did not have red battery-lights attached to their lifejackets.

There were several individual acts of heroism, like the member of *Hydrangea's* crew who, on seeing a man feebly waving in the dark, went over the side into the water on a bowline in an endeavour to sling a line around him. But the surface of the sea was covered in oil fuel and the Norwegian's clothing was completely saturated with it; he was also so exhausted that he was a dead weight, and each time the bowline was slung around him and an attempt made to hoist him from the water, the line slipped from his body. For a full fifteen minutes the *Hydrangea* sailor fought to save the man, until with a last faint cry he slipped away and was lost again in the darkness.

It was 3 a.m. before the last half-dead survivor was won from the water by *Hydrangea's* boat. The corvette had saved more than forty men, though a number of these were very seriously injured. *Wanderer* had saved another four.

Less than fifty men in all — and *Bath* had carried nearly 130. Her captain was among the missing.

Minutes after *Bath* was hit, a second surfaced U-boat coming up astern had found a victim among the merchantmen. Kapitanleutnant Hans Heidtmann in U-559 had celebrated his twenty-seventh birthday only a few days before. Now he determined to mark it with a good kill. A torpedo from U-559 sped towards the ss. *Alva*.

Chief Officer Speller was on watch on the *Alva*, a Glasgow ship carrying 2,000 tons of coal, when he looked astern, saw a distant flash and heard the far-off explosion as *Bath* was smashed in two. Less than ten minutes later the torpedo from U-559 smacked into *Alva* forward of the bridge in the way of No. 3 hold on the starboard side. Clouds of coal dust shot into the air as the explosion severely damaged the starboard side of the bridge, blew off all the No. 3 hatches and reduced the liferaft on the foredeck to fragments.

Speller rang the engine-room telegraph to 'Stop' but the engines had stopped even as he did so. The master, Captain Palmer, hurried to join him on the damaged bridge. Already the ship was listing heavily to starboard and he ordered Speller to get the boats cleared away. Speller also went to fire the emergency signal rockets but found that these had been blown away. There was a boat's emergency set in the chart-room but this whole room had been destroyed in the explosion. In a few minutes the master and crew — *Alva* carried twenty-five, including five naval gunners — knew that the ship was doomed. She was settling rapidly. Captain Palmer gave the order to abandon ship.

The starboard boat was got away without difficulty in a westerly swell, some other men taking to the remaining two liferafts. The captain, after throwing the ship's confidential books overboard in a weighted bag, scrambled to join his chief officer and the men in the second boat, and this too hurriedly cast off.

Just two minutes later, at 1.35 a.m., they watched the dark shape of the shattered *Alva* slide beneath the surface. They lighted a red flare and were relieved to see a vessel loom up in the dark after only fifteen minutes. She was the Eire ship *Clonlara*. Her master, Captain Reynolds, had reduced speed and gone full astern to effect a rescue. Now, regardless of the danger, he stopped his vessel for half an hour to pick up survivors.

Clonlara was joined in her mercy work by the *Empire Oak*, the crew of the steam tug using white cotton heaving lines to pick up other survivors of *Alva*, who gratefully saw the ropes fairly easily in the darkness. Although there now was a big sea running, the rescue work went ahead without mishap except for minor injuries. The two vessels each took on about half of *Alva's* crew, Captain Palmer and Chief Officer Speller being in the party picked up by *Clonlara*.

It was 2.30 a.m. when, the last survivor having been hauled on board, *Clonlara* and *Empire Oak* put on all speed to catch up the convoy.

Miles behind them at this time, at the grim scene of RNN *Bath's* dreadful end, the corvette *Hydrangea* was saving the last Norwegian sailors from the sea. So badly injured were some of them that the destroyer *Wanderer* had to go alongside and pass over her medical officer to attend to them. Both ships remained to search the sea till daylight but to no avail; there was no one else left alive, only some silently floating bodies, here and there a piece of wreckage, and lingering patches of oil on the sea.

On the first news of the attack at the rear of the convoy, its exact details unknown, Captain Frith ordered *Aguila's* passengers to stand by, all lifejackets to be worn. He also sent orders to the Wrens that they were not to go to bed in their cabins but must stay together in what had been in happier days the ship's library, next to the boatdeck. After an hour or more had passed without further alarm he relaxed these instructions and sent word to the passengers that they could go to their respective cabins and lie down, but not to undress, and with the warning to be ready to go to their allotted emergency stations immediately the alarm was sounded.

At 3 a.m. the convoy made a pre-arranged change of course to 162 degrees and Captain Frith remained on the bridge with Commodore Parker until *Aguila* was steady on her new course. Parker then suggested that the master take the opportunity of going below for a rest. Captain Frith gratefully retired to his room, partly undressed, and lay down on the settee to close his weary eyes.

Over on the Vice-Commodore ship *Ciscar*, leading one of the other columns of merchantmen, they too had heard the distant explosion as *Bath* was hit and seen searching starshell being fired by escorts. They could not be sure whether the enemy's new attack had come from the air or the sea, but Captain Hughes assumed it to be a torpedo attack and took no chances; he ordered everyone on deck, lifejackets to be worn, guns manned, and had the boats made ready with blankets and survival equipment. The *Ciscar* also carried five rafts which lay free on the deck in complete readiness, the master making it a practice never to lash them except in bad weather.

Although as the night wore on the emergency receded and the gun crews stood down, the ship remained on the alert. Then came the 3 a.m. change of course, perfectly executed; but also perfectly followed by Kapitanleutnant Adalbert Schnee's U-201 which had stealthily overtaken the convoy on the port flank. Schnee loosed his torpedoes.

Captain Hughes was standing on the starboard side of the

bridge when a torpedo tore into *Ciscar's* engine-room on the port side. There was no flash, just a dull, shuddering explosion followed by a strong smell of cordite. Debris and splinters showered down on the captain as he started to run over to the port side of the bridge, only to find that it had been blown away. Three seconds later a second torpedo struck the ship further aft in No. 4 hold. Again there was no flash and only a muffled explosion among the government stores, but the hatch covers and beams were blasted sky high and a seaman walking past at the time was blown fifty feet into the air and hurled into the water (surprisingly he survived to be picked up later). The four-inch gun aft was hurled to one side and the gunners' quarters in the 'tween deck of No. 4 hold wrecked, killing instantly the four gunners in there. *Ciscar* at once started to list to port.

The ship's second officer ran out of the chart-room, a gunner followed him, then the man who had been at the wheel, and the master shouted after the three of them to get on to a raft lying on top of the hatch near the bridge, for the ship was going down by the stern as she rapidly heeled over ninety degrees. Captain Hughes himself jumped over the top of the wheelhouse to the other side and grabbed hold of another raft — just in time. Two seconds later *Ciscar* sank under him and he was in the water.

The ship had disappeared within forty-five seconds of being hit.

As the vessel went down the suction was so great that the captain was unable to hold on to his raft and was dragged down ten fathoms deep before he could begin to fight his way up again, fully clothed and lungs bursting. On reaching the surface he found himself about ten feet from the raft, but although he swam towards it for what seemed ages he could not reach it, a light breeze on the water blowing it away from him faster than he could swim. He eventually managed to grab hold of a floating hatch cover, which turned over crazily in the water four or five times before he could find a suitable position for hanging on to it.

Ciscar had sunk so quickly that there had been no time to fire an emergency rocket, and she had gone so quietly that hardly any other ship in the convoy could be aware of her fate. As Captain Hughes struggled to hang on to his life-saving hatch cover in the dark, choppy sea he heard a loud explosion. Had another ship been hit?

It had.

More of U-201's torpedoes sped to intercept the biggish

three-masted ship leading the fourth column of merchant vessels. The Commodore ship.

After the 3 a.m. change of course, followed by the temporary departure of Captain Frith from the bridge of *Aguila* as she steamed steadily on, Yeoman of Signals Fred Buckingham nevertheless still felt uneasy. He decided to remain up and told his leading signalman that he could turn in.

Buckingham then left the bridge briefly to go between decks to the heads. While there he felt an explosion. He asked an RN lieutenant standing alongside him if he had felt it, but the officer replied he had not.

Buckingham cut short and hurried back to the bridge where, in reply to his question, they all, including the Commodore, said they had heard nothing — such had been the quick and almost noiseless demise of *Ciscar*.

But they had little time to dwell on the yeoman's puzzling experience. Within seconds a torpedo hit *Aguila* amidships on the port side in the stoke-hole, shaking the ship violently. Buckingham momentarily froze with his back against the wheelhouse in case any of the sacks of sand on its roof should be dislodged by the explosion and fall. Then, before he or anyone else could move, a second torpedo struck again on the port side in the engine-room, slightly abaft the first one, extinguishing all the ship's lights and plunging them into darkness.

The helmsman stumbled out of the wheelhouse, spoke briefly to the officer on watch and jumped over the side into the sea. Yeoman Buckingham ran across to the starboard side of the bridge, opened a small box, took out the Convoy Signal Book, placed it in a weighted canvas bag with his other confidential books, zipped it shut and threw it over the side. He then ran down the ladder to the lower bridge, intending to fire an emergency rocket, but he never reached it. The ship had broken in half and now sank at once, and he with it.

At the impact of the first torpedo Captain Frith, who had just laid down to rest on the settee in his state-room under the bridge, was nearly flung to the floor. He scrambled up, but before he could get to the door the second torpedo struck, putting out the lights. He rushed out of his room and practically stepped into the frothing sea. Seeing that the broken ship was plunging down fast he jumped straight on to a raft which floated off the fore end of the promenade deck.

Assistant Steward Harold Hughes just managed to get to the same raft. At the first explosion Hughes had seen the main staircase from the lounge to the main deck collapse in a mass of flames. As the second torpedo struck, blasting out the ship's lights, he had struggled to help a Wren up to the promenade deck in the dark but lost her as the vessel foundered. Now Hughes and the master, clinging on to the raft, were both pulled under by the suction of the *Aguila* sinking fast like a descending escalator, Captain Frith taking a severe knock in the back from a piece of timber as they went. They kicked themselves free and spluttered choking to the surface close to the raft, which dizzily turned over and over in the water. They fought to trap it and finally struggled on to it.

Aguila had vanished in ninety seconds.

Yeoman Buckingham, sucked down as *Aguila* sank, started swimming, he hoped, to the surface when he was hit underwater by the shrouds of the ship's foremast and taken down even further. He desperately curled himself up into a ball, allowing the shrouds to spin him free, which left him clear to start for the surface again. During this long, lung-bursting time under water he had only one thought: if he wasn't swimming straight up he was going to die, and his wife of a few days would be a widow.

On gasping to the surface he found himself in the hub of a 'spinning wheel', the circumference of the wheel being a lot of lights, some electric, some acetylene. He waited for the spinning to stop, meanwhile struggling out of duffle coat and jacket. His seaboots, which he had no recollection of loosening, must have come off as soon as he entered the water. When the spinning subsided he started to swim towards one of the acetylene lights which he knew would be attached to a large lifesaving raft.

While swimming in the dark he heard someone splashing and moaning and came upon another survivor, a young ship's steward, who was clearly in a state of shock. Buckingham helped to guide him towards the raft.

The steward, David Kerr, aged only nineteen, had gone to his bunk after the concert in the saloon with the finale by the Wrens. One of his regular duties had been to serve meals to eight of the Wrens, as he had done that evening before the concert. The girls had made a big impression on him, all so cheerful and obviously thrilled at leaving Blighty for service overseas, talking animatedly about what life in Gib would be like. He had turned in, his lifejacket over his clothes, with 'The World Is Waiting For The Sunrise' still ringing tunefully in his ears.

The next thing he knew was finding himself awake and afloat in the sea in utter darkness, unable to grasp what had happened or how he had got there. Cries for help came from all directions out of the night, adding to his confusion as he pitched and bobbed in the disturbed water. He could distinguish among them the cries of a girl or girls, but could see nothing. Floating helplessly he felt himself being lifted on a heavy swell and became aware that he was clutching under his right arm a baulk of timber, which evidently had saved him from drowning. The cries of others in the water now became fainter and he thought to himself, 'My God! What if the swell is carrying me away? I could be miles away from the scene by the time the rescue ships arrive. I would be alive and afloat, but *alone* in this seemingly endless ocean. . . .'

The thought terrified him. He must act. Seeing a faint light flickering on the water, rising and falling in the swell, he reasoned that it must be coming from a raft, pushed the piece of timber away and started out for the light. But suddenly the distance seemed too great, he panicked, threshed back and retrieved the timber. Then, recovering his nerve after a brief rest, he pushed it away again and struck out wearily . . . until Yeoman Buckingham appeared beside him and guided him to the raft.

Kerr's escape, it was later established, was nothing short of miraculous. What happened was that he had been asleep in his bunk when the explosion from the first torpedo blew him out into the companionway and the second explosion hurled him up the ladder into the sea. His legs now seemed paralysed, only later would it be discovered that they were both broken, his spine and jaw fractured.

The raft joined by Buckingham and Kerr was the one found by Captain Frith and Steward Hughes, who had also dragged on board two seamen they found clinging to wreckage. Another occupant of the raft — there were seven in all, including the new arrivals — was an officers' steward who had been at a temporary urinal by the mainmast when the ship was struck, and had run up the mast and just floated off when the ship sank.

Yeoman Buckingham had by instinct checked his watch when the first torpedo hit *Aguila*. It struck the ship at 3.10 a.m. Now he checked again and found that his watch had stopped at 3.11 $\frac{1}{2}$ a.m. — the exact second that *Aguila* went down and he battled to be free of her.

No other survivors reached the captain's raft but, unseen across the water, another, smaller raft had got clear.

Leading Aircraft Mechanic William Churchouse of the Fleet Air Arm had been on passage in *Aguila* to join the aircraft carrier *Ark Royal* at Gibraltar. When the first torpedo struck the ship he was flung from his bunk in cabin 48 on the bridge deck. He had placed his lifejacket carefully near by in case of an emergency but the force of the explosion dislodged it, and in the darkness and confusion following the second explosion almost immediately afterwards he was unable to find it.

He ran out on to the upper deck and tried to make his way in the dark to the boat deck, but found that the companionway had been blown away and there was no means of getting to the boats. He turned to run back to his cabin and make another attempt to find his lifejacket but was met by a wall of water as the ship's stern disappeared fast under the sea.

He was drawn down with the dying ship, struggling against swirling debris, and injured his foot in fortunately coming to the surface through the blown-off hatch of the promenade deck. Then the ship had gone and he was left swimming in the dark among coal dust and debris.

None of the boats had got away, there had not been time, but Churchouse saw a calcium flare and swam to it. The light came from a small liferaft and he was helped on to it by the occupants, both of whom were seamen who had been on watch when the ship sank. As the three men huddled on the raft they could hear cries for help but were unable to give assistance as they could see little in the dark and the lop of the sea. It was as much as they could do to try to keep themselves afloat.

The corvette HMS *Wallflower* steamed to the rescue.

First, she found Captain Frith's raft, guided by its light and Yeoman Buckingham's blasts on his whistle. The exhausted men were helped on board. Steward David Kerr, as he tried to follow the others up the Jacob's ladder, discovered for the first time that he couldn't stand up and had to be hauled bodily on board, where examination revealed his broken limbs. Even in his own considerable misery, however, the first question on the lad's lips was, had any of the Wrens been saved? When heads were shaken he felt a shudder of horror at the girls lost in the awful waste of water and darkness.

Wallflower afterwards came upon the smaller raft on which William Churchouse and the two crewmen of *Aguila* were adrift. The Fleet Air Arm man wore only vest and pants and was by this time suffering greatly from the cold, having to be helped shivering up the scrambling net by strong arms.

While *Wallflower* continued to probe the sea, hoping to find more survivors, she was screened by *Campanula*, who fired off starshell both to illuminate the search area and to reveal any lurking U-boat.

Captain F.E. Christian of the *Empire Oak*, which had put on steam to catch up the convoy after picking up half of the survivors from the sunken *Alva*, saw the starshell going up, and as the tug neared the position he spotted a number of lights in the water which he took to be the red lights attached to merchantmen's lifejackets. He manoeuvred *Empire Oak* towards the lights until they were alongside and his crew could give the maximum help. They picked up four seamen from *Aguila* struggling in the water. They also found the ship's chief officer, who was a rather heavy man, on a small raft trying to give aid to a distraught seaman suffering from a broken thigh. They got the pair safely on board and continued the search. But neither the tug nor *Wallflower* could find another living soul, despite searching long and hard in the darkness.

Meanwhile in the confusion another of the escort corvettes, HMS *Campion*, had a frighteningly narrow escape when four torpedoes were suddenly seen to cross her bow from port to starboard. 'Full ahead, hard to port, steadied ship in torpedoes' wake. . . .' was the cool record by *Campion's* captain of an extremely close shave. But the good thing about it was that the enemy had wasted four more 'tinfish'. It seemed to be his parting shot of the night for no further sign of him could be traced.

The survivors of ss. *Ciscar*, torpedoed shortly before *Aguila*, were passed in the dark by two ships before a third answered their hoarse cries and stopped to pick them up. The ss. *Petrel* lowered two boats and was stopped for over two hours while her crew searched the choppy waters.

Nine members of *Ciscar's* crew had been saved by the rafts which had floated free when the ship sank in forty-five seconds, but the rest had only time to jump over the side and swim hard to avoid being sucked under with her. All were wearing lifejackets fitted with red lights, but several of these lights failed to work, which made things doubly difficult for the rescuers, guided only by men's cries.

Top: Captain Arthur Frith, master of the Commodore ship *Aguila*.
Above Left: Commodore's Yeoman of Signals Fred Buckingham.
Above Right: Leading Aircraft Mechanic William Churchouse of the Fleet Air Arm, on passage in *Aguila* to join the aircraft carrier *Ark Royal*.

Photo: U.S. National Archiv[es]

Above: The World War 1 destroyer USS. *Hopewell* in the 1920s: she was one of a package of 50 old destroyers given to Britain for the new war.
Below: How four-stacker *Hopewell* looked in her new guise as RNN *Bath*, escort convoy OG71.

Photo: Royal Norwegian Na[vy]

Being all fully clothed the survivors floated up to their necks in the sea which had a nasty chop on it, making it difficult to breathe as the waves washed over them. Captain Hughes, struggling almost fully immersed like the rest of his men, had to hold the red light from his lifejacket in his hand with his arm out of the water, otherwise it could not have been seen. Through having to hold up the light in the angry sea he unfortunately lost it, and it was over two and a half hours before he was found, being among the last of *Ciscar's* half-drowned company to be fished exhausted from the sea.

Petrel's boats did a good job, picking up twenty-five survivors in all, including the master; but thirteen of *Ciscar's* company had been lost.

As *Petrel* steamed to rejoin the convoy she was escorted by *Wallflower*, who had now been forced to abandon her fruitless search for more survivors of *Aguila*.

At this same time, miles away to the rear, corvette *Hydrangea* and destroyer *Wanderer* had also broken off their long, vain search for more survivors of *Bath*.

7.10 a.m. In a calm morning sea *Hydrangea* set about transferring thirty-five survivors of *Bath* to the destroyer, retaining on board another eleven seriously-injured men who could not be moved. Sadly, despite the best efforts of *Wanderer's* medical officer who remained with the corvette, two of the wounded, one a Norwegian rating and one British, died even as the transfer was going on.

The two ships now parted company. Even carrying the seriously wounded, it was considered essential for *Hydrangea* to rejoin the convoy and resume her escort duties, while *Wanderer* turned for home with the other thirty-five survivors. She had just sufficient fuel to reach her base of Lough Foyle, Londonderry, providing the weather did not deteriorate.

Hydrangea, steaming at fifteen knots to catch up the convoy, stopped just before noon to bury the two survivors of *Bath* who had died. Their bodies were cast to the deep with full naval honours, their only epitaph being the position of their Atlantic grave entered in the ship's log: 48 degrees 34 minutes North, 17 degrees 39 minutes West.

Soon afterwards *Hydrangea* overtook and passed HMS *Wallflower* escorting the slower *Petrel*.

The grim news of the night's events came piecemeal to the

escort leader, *Leith*, from ships involved, the sloop then signalling the bare facts to Admiralty, as destroyer *Wanderer* had done earlier regarding *Bath*.

Four ships sunk. The escort destroyer *Bath*, with great loss of life. The Commodore ship *Aguila*, with the appalling loss of almost all her passengers and crew including the Commodore himself — only sixteen known survivors, including the master, out of a company of 161. And the Vice-Commodore ship *Ciscar*, and the *Alva* . . .

As the convoy continued on its southerly course *Empire Oak* and *Petrel* both signalled for *Leith's* doctor to attend to the more seriously-injured survivors. He was eventually swung on board each vessel in turn in a moderate sea, but earlier treatment had had to be managed by the various ships' crews to the best of their ability.

On board *Wallflower*, Able Seaman David McDonald and a stoker had volunteered to help tend the wounded, who were carried to the seamen's mess and laid out on the messdeck tables. Some had shin bones protruding through the flesh, some had rib bones protruding and broken. McDonald had never rendered first-aid in his life; the only medical instruction he had been given was on the sixteen pressure points to stop bleeding, the one thing that all corvette crews were taught. There was morphine available but McDonald did not know how to use it; instead, with the captain's permission, he replenished a teapot with neat rum from the rum jar and made each survivor drink a cupful. Some who never drank alcohol only managed to get half a cup down after much coaxing, but after that they were beyond caring. With a broken limb, McDonald would hold the leg above the break, pull the foot, and the bone would disappear into the flesh. Then he lined it up with the other broken part until it was smooth to the thumb, and on with a splint. With broken ribs little could be done except to dress and bandage up the wound. Then into bed in bunks given up by members of the crew, McDonald making a kind of 'tent' out of splints to keep the clothes and weight of the blanket off a man's wound.

On board *Clonlara*, Chief Officer Speller of *Alva*, who had been rescued along with his captain and some of the crew, trained his glasses on *Empire Oak* and recognised other *Alva* survivors on board her. He signalled across to the tug and after a general 'roll call' found that only one man, the cook, was missing. They had been very lucky.

Information was passed between other ships. It was thought

and hoped that the tug might have saved some of the Wrens. Only the previous evening the girls had been seen waving happily from the deck of *Aguila*; now they and their ship had gone. It was a dreadful, unbelievable loss. Reports of survivors of all four ships were still very unclear as the convoy pressed on, *Leith* having appointed the ss. *Spero*, a small vessel carrying general cargo, to take over the duties of Commodore ship.

What did seem clear now was that the convoy was being closely shadowed, that enemy aircraft had 'homed in' the U-boats. Confirmation of this came during the afternoon when a Junkers 88 and two Focke-Wulfs were sighted for long periods. The planes kept their distance, making no attempt to attack, the last Focke-Wulf circling until dusk.

But help was at hand. On receiving the first reports of the devastating night attack on OG71 the C-in-C Western Approaches (Admiral Sir Percy Noble) had acted. He signalled two long-range escort destroyers screening convoy WS10X, far west of Ireland, to detach forthwith, steam at speed for OG71 and proceed with the convoy to Gibraltar. 'U-boats have attacked convoy and may be in vicinity,' warned the C-in-C's signal.

The two destroyers, HMS *Gurkha* and HMS *Lance*, were big, modern 2,000-ton warships. *Gurkha*, the senior vessel, captained by Commander C.N. Lentaigne, was fitted with advanced high frequency radio-direction-finding equipment which could intercept enemy transmissions from land, sea and in the air; and, most importantly, aided by cross-bearings from *Lance*, could in favourable conditions pinpoint transmitting surfaced U-boats at great distance. This was a tremendous advantage, for the corvettes were not yet fitted with the early type of sea radar then available. Their asdic underwater detector could only detect a submerged enemy and was virtually useless against U-boats operating on the surface; they were restricted to visual sighting, hence the best they could do on escort duty was to zig-zag erratically around the convoy as a physical barrier, trying to impede the enemy's attacks.

For some time now, under the tactics introduced by Admiral Karl Doenitz, commander-in-chief of the U-boat fleet, German submarines had taken to operating more on the surface, and at night, when a U-boat's small, low shape was difficult to spot in the darkness by ships' lookouts on the high bridges of naval and merchant ships. Moreover, a surfaced U-boat had the legs of a corvette which, with a maximum speed of sixteen knots, had no chance of overhauling it; a surfaced U-boat could travel at eighteen knots and more. Even the convoy escort's leader, the sloop *Leith*, was unable to match that speed.

Gurkha had both the speed and the means of surface detection, in addition to asdic. With a tripod aerial foremast, a strange structure looking very like a pylon tower situated behind the bridge and standing twice the height of her funnel, she was something special for her time. Her name was special, too. She had begun life as the *Larne* but was renamed *Gurkha* after a Tribal-class destroyer of that name was sunk in the Norwegian campaign; the Gurkha regiments had subscribed a day's pay per man to replace her.

Gurkha and *Lance* parted company from WS10X at noon and steamed at a fast twenty-two knots to join OG71, their estimated time of arrival being soon after midnight.

At sunset, as they sped after the convoy, *Gurkha* commenced her listening search and at 10 p.m. obtained second-class bearings on at least one transmitting U-boat, which indicated that the convoy was indeed still being shadowed.

5
MORE WOLVES TO THE KILL

5

MORE WOLVES TO THE KILL

WEDNESDAY 20 August. The day was only minutes old when, still searching the airwaves while steaming through heavy rain, *Gurkha's* RDF detected another 'possible' U-boat. She and *Lance* accordingly narrowed their course and put on speed to overtake the convoy at the earliest hour.

They arrived within a few miles of OG71 soon after 3 a.m. Simultaneously a strong U-boat contact was obtained by *Gurkha* but lost in the heavy sea, the German had probably dived on seeing them approach.

Gurkha's captain, Commander Lentaigne, slackened speed, sending *Lance* forward to close with the convoy and carry out a search along its port flank, across the stern and down the starboard flank at a distance of four miles.

Lentaigne's intention after this precautionary sweep was to place his two destroyers between the U-boats and the convoy as the sun rose, so that *Gurkha* would be able to detect any marauder coming in to attack at daybreak.

Sounds were heard of an aircraft passing over the convoy in the dark sky, and shortly afterwards the RDF also picked up signals of another unseen plane. Later, after *Lance's* exhaustive search around the convoy and with the two destroyers standing well off astern, cross-bearings gave a U-boat only two miles to the north. It was very, very tempting to give chase, but with bad asdic conditions, no further RDF contact and the near certainty that other U-boats were out there, it was clear to Lentaigne that their first duty was to stay close and protect the convoy. This decision was endorsed when RDF detected the presence of another unseen aircraft.

Gurkha closed with corvette *Wallflower* at the rear of the convoy and Lentaigne learned what little was known of the events of the previous night. Lentaigne now was the most senior naval officer on the scene, but he sent *Lance* ahead to tell the captain of *Leith*, leading the convoy, to remain as senior officer of the close escort, the sloop alone having all the information about OG71 now that both the Commodore and Vice-Commodore ships had been sunk. This would allow *Gurkha* and *Lance* to act independently as an outer screen of anti-aircraft escorts by day and a fast anti-submarine striking force by night. There was, however, one drawback in that the stay of both destroyers was limited: they each had only a certain amount of fuel left and would have to leave the convoy at the latest on the afternoon of the 23rd to steam on to Gibraltar and fuel up.

The pair now stationed themselves astern of the convoy, watchful for any enemy attack.

The destroyers' arrival came as a particular relief to Lieutenant Woolfenden, commanding the corvette *Hydrangea*. The critical condition of the nine wounded survivors of *Bath* she was carrying was a great worry. Now that the escort had been strengthened he asked permission of *Leith* to leave the convoy and proceed at best speed for Gibraltar. *Leith's* commander, knowing that the destroyers would have to leave after three days, declined to let him go, but only an hour after Woolfenden's request had been refused another of the *Bath* survivors, her Norwegian second lieutenant, died. Woolfenden now despaired for the lives of some of the others, but timely intervention came in the form of a signal from C-in-C WA, stating that if the condition of the remaining survivors warranted, *Hydrangea* could detach and make for Gibraltar at once.

Leith's commander now agreed, and shortly after noon Woolfenden thankfully left the convoy and steamed *Hydrangea* for Gibraltar at her maximum speed of sixteen knots. Some three hours out on her journey she again stopped briefly to make a burial at sea, the Norwegian officer being accorded full honours. Then on at full engines for the Rock, which, at more than twice the speed of the convoy, she could hopefully expect to reach within two days.

Back with the convoy, sailing through a rough and very mist-ridden sea, *Gurkha* sighted a shadowing Focke-Wulf at seven miles distance. The plane, flying low over the water, vanished into the mist again, then fleetingly reappeared, apparently hugging every bank of mist in an attempt to close in on the convoy. *Gurkha* and *Lance* opened fire as soon as there was range and kept firing whenever the plane tried to manoeuvre closer in to obtain a target. Eventually the German pilot seemed to abandon his idea of a bombing attack but remained at a safe distance, continuing to shadow and make homing signals during the afternoon until flying off.

In the evening the mist suddenly lifted to expose the convoy lumbering along in a clear twilight sea, a revealing sight for determined hunters. Commander Lentaigne signalled *Leith* that a drastic alteration of course was necessary to put the enemy off the scent. This was agreed and *Gurkha* and *Lance* dropped back again to screen the convoy from any shadowers coming up astern.

The night, however, remained quiet, except for one angry incident. Both of the Eire vessels had proved lax with their blackout precautions, lights on board them being seen from time to time despite frequent warnings. When *Clonlara* yet again exposed a tell-tale shaft of light from an ill-covered doorway the exasperated captain of corvette *Campion* speedily closed on the vessel and fired a warning shot.

'*Clonlara*,' he hailed, 'you are persistently showing lights. If you don't put them out we will fire into you!' He repeated the message to show that he was in deadly earnest.

Captain Reynolds hastily acknowledged the warning and went round his ship to inspect the blackouts and find the offending aperture. Unlike the British ships, the Limerick vessel had not been supplied with proper blackout arrangements, the only cut-out door switches fitted being those on the master's own cabin door and that of the saloon. The crew had been left to find their own material and makeshift methods of screening off any lights elsewhere in the ship and were very casual about it, as the survivors she was carrying had found.

Next day *Clonlara* would be ordered to change her position from outside ship in the starboard column into the centre column, where she would be less of a hazard and under the wary eye of fellow merchant skippers on either side.

Thursday 21 August. The night passed uneventfully, but during the morning several enemy transmissions were intercepted by *Gurkha* and at noon a distant U-boat was detected sending messages. Shortly afterwards another welcome reinforcement for the convoy arrived, the patrolling destroyer HMS *Boreas*. *Gurkha's* commander ordered her to take up a position on the convoy's starboard quarter and keep a good U-boat lookout.

The blue morning sky was empty of fellow travellers, but with depressing inevitability another shadowing Focke-Wulf was sighted low down on the north-eastern horizon during the afternoon. When *Gurkha* opened fire it flew out of sight, though whether it had gone altogether no one could be sure. The convoy immediately zig-zagged, while the outer escorts, now including *Boreas*, made a thorough anti-submarine search.

The early evening brought a sudden flurry of enemy wireless activity, *Gurkha* obtaining a series of RDF bearings from the south, south-west and west. From it all, it was deduced that the enemy had not yet regained contact with the convoy although he probably had a very shrewd idea of its position. There seemed to be at least five U-boats spread out on a rough line of bearing parallel to the convoy at a distance of about fifteen miles.

Commander Lentaigne now had to decide whether to leave the convoy and go after the 'wolf-pack' on an offensive night sweep, or to remain with his charges and take evasive action. He decided on the latter course, coming up with a simple ruse. After nightfall he would detach a corvette to steam north-west for two hours, carry out a mock battle at midnight and then steam at full speed to the east, turning to rejoin the convoy at dawn. It was hoped that German D/F stations would intercept the corvette's signals and confirm her position to be that of the convoy. This would induce the prowling U-boats to turn northwards to investigate, while the convoy would in fact steer 110 degrees through the night and later alter course to the south, so putting itself as far ahead of the wolves as possible.

Lentaigne further gambled that the U-boats, on failing to find the convoy, would assume it had passed to the north-west of them during the night and accordingly continue to search in that direction until enemy shadowing aircraft, if they returned, refound OG71 next day and reported its proper position.

The corvette chosen to put on the 'firework display' was HMS *Bluebell*. She duly left the convoy at 10 p.m.

Her performance was anxiously awaited on board *Gurkha*, the time seeming to move extraordinarily slowly. Then, precisely at midnight, the sea some forty miles away to the north-east was lit up as *Bluebell* launched into an enthusiastic and highly convincing display as ordered. For ten minutes she 'fought' her mock battle, firing starshell, dropping depth-charges, busily transmitting and making an immediate signal to Admiralty and C-in-C WA (signing the signal 'Gurkha') giving her position and stating: 'OG71 being shadowed by six U-boats and aircraft. Urgently request air support from dawn.'

Then, her job done, she silently sped off eastwards into the night.

Friday 22 August. After *Bluebell* had finished her fireworks there were more tense minutes of waiting on board *Gurkha*. Then, at half past midnight, the enemy was suddenly busy and the destroyer began to pick up signals. Bearings confirmed that at least four U-boats were now moving northwards to investigate. The trick appeared to have worked. *Gurkha's* tired RDF operators could afford to relax and raise a cheer.

The rest of the night was peaceful, *Bluebell* rejoining the convoy at dawn exactly as planned. On *Gurkha*, soon after the corvette's return, an RDF interception of the enemy, much farther distant than any previously obtained, confirmed that the mock battle had been entirely successful and the bamboozled Germans were still searching in that area.

A welcome sight at breakfast time was the arrival of another Catalina. But *Gurkha* found she could not make contact with the flying boat by either radio-telephony or wireless-telegraph, and only very occasionally, and with unusual difficulty, by visual signalling. This was a blow, for the consequent delays in passing signals to the aeroplane ruined the chances of a good air search assisted by the destroyer's RDF.

9.40 a.m. Commander Lentaigne's assumption that, despite the night's diversion, enemy shadowers would eventually find the convoy again was proved well founded when two Focke-Wulfs were sighted. The Catalina boldly remained flying in their vicinity but had insufficient speed to menace them. For their part, the enemy planes made no move to attack. They clearly had other intentions.

The convoy altered course but the shadowing aircraft remained. Very soon *Gurkha* detected them making wireless calls and apparently being answered by U-boats giving their call signs. *Gurkha* and *Boreas* threw up a fierce barrage of ack-ack fire when the planes flew in closer but they simply retreated out of range.

Gurkha's commander now signalled the Catalina to fly off and try to keep down the transmitting U-boats. This it did with some reluctance in view of the presence of the enemy planes, which it considered its duty to harass. Lentaigne then ordered *Lance* to steam five miles eastward and with constant fire from her A/A guns try to keep the aircraft well distant from the convoy, so as to reduce the strength of their signals to the U-boats and prevent accurate homing. But in spite of a determined show by *Lance* the enemy wireless activity continued to build up.

More help came at midday when the destroyer HMS *Wivern*, an older, short-range escort, was sighted to the west. Lentaigne stationed her six miles from the convoy while *Lance* and *Boreas* steamed off to hunt a detected U-boat.

A bleak signal from Admiralty now reached the escorts: 'Wireless traffic from U-boats suggests there are up to nine U-boats in your general vicinity.'

1 p.m. The two Focke-Wulfs ceased transmitting and flew off, but on board *Gurkha* the picture was not good, the Admiralty's signal only confirming the destroyer's own findings. From her RDF interceptions it was now believed that there were at least eight U-boats present, some of them not far below the horizon. *Lance*, *Boreas* and *Wivern* were sent off again to hunt. So was the Catalina, which returned in mid-afternoon without having seen a thing.

At this juncture the big steamer *Marklyn* broke down and stopped with engine defects. Corvette *Campanula* was detached to stand by her while the convoy carried on; it could not slacken speed now.

A second Catalina then appeared. This plane too did not carry R/T but to the relief of *Gurkha's* captain it did have W/T and was speedily sent off to conduct a twenty-mile search. It had scarcely gone when two Junkers 88s attacked out of the sun. Their target was the straggled *Marklyn* which, her engines righted, had just started up to rejoin the convoy. At 3,000 tons and, in ballast, high in the water, she offered a prime target, but surprisingly both hurtling sticks of bombs missed, the Junkers afterwards making off unscathed despite strong retaliatory fire from *Gurkha*, *Campanula* and the merchant ship herself.

An hour later a U-boat was detected at eight miles. *Boreas* and *Wivern* continued to search, meanwhile the Catalina returned to report that it had forced a U-boat to dive twenty-five miles from the convoy.

7 p.m. After the busy and threatening events of the day, with *Gurkha's* RDF staff working at full stretch, Commander Lentaigne now had to plan tactics for another long night. The situation was that six, possibly seven, U-boats had been detected at varying distances from the convoy. It was decided to alter the course of OG71 at midnight, then back again in the early morning. Before the change of course Lentaigne would hope to drive the U-boats back, and possibly sight one or more of them, by *Gurkha*, *Lance*, *Boreas*, and *Wivern* together making a vigorous sweep to the west for fifteen miles, returning afterwards to form an outer screen three miles from the convoy. During the destroyers' fast sweep the corvettes were to remain with the convoy and send up illuminating snowflake rockets; also, at their captains' discretion, firing starshell to help the destroyers at long range; in this way the sea for a considerable area would be lit up and finely swept, exposing the cleverest skulking enemy.

9 p.m. The two Catalinas, now low on fuel, left the convoy and the four destroyers began their offensive sweep, firing starshell and raking the sea with searchlights on each flank of the convoy before spreading out to three miles apart in line abreast and steaming forward in unison at a pugnacious eighteen knots. *Gurkha* obtained several contacts at short range but these transpired to be probably waves or boxes in the water, for although course was altered to close on the echoes nothing was seen. Unfortunately only one snowflake rocket was fired by one of the corvettes — the others had run out of them — which prevented the hoped-for total area of revealing illumination between the convoy and the destroyers.

At the end of the sweep the four destroyers turned as one to rejoin the convoy. *Gurkha*, directly after turning, for good measure released two great smoke clouds which remained in sight for a distance of nine miles. Lentaigne hoping that they might divert and delay any surfaced U-boat coming into position to attack. Minutes later two transmitting U-boats were detected but could not be accurately plotted.

Soon it would be time for the convoy to make its change of course. It now progressed steadily through the dark sea, *Leith* at its head, the corvettes at their positions on each flank and the destroyers bringing up the rear.

But in spite of all the searching and skirmishing one of the enemy submarines had found a way through. Oberleutnant-zur-See Reinhard Suhren had 'homed in' U-564 perfectly on the starboard flank. At the age of twenty-five, Suhren was a skilled submariner commanding his second U-boat, and already a holder of the Knight's Cross of the Iron Cross. The torpedoes he now sent into the convoy, angled so that if they missed one ship they would be bound to hit another, claimed two more victims to add to his growing tally of kills.

Captain Christian of the *Empire Oak* was standing on the starboard wing of his bridge when one of Suhren's torpedoes struck the tug on the starboard side in the engine-room. There was a shock impact, followed by a great flash and explosion which threw up a huge column of water that obliterated everything from sight as it descended on the bridge. As the drenching water cleared, the master saw the ship's funnel fall crazily over one side of the vessel and the mainmast over the other. The tug's back had been instantly broken and in seconds she suddenly dropped below the surface as if a hole in the ocean had opened beneath her, the captain being washed off the bridge and sucked down with her. He was wearing his lifejacket and beat his way up to the surface just in time to see ten feet of his ship's bow standing perpendicular above the water, then this too disappeared as he swam to keep afloat in the flurried sea.

Across the convoy Chief Officer Speller, survivor from *Alva*, had volunteered to keep watch on the bridge of the Eire coalship *Clonlara*, now sailing almost in the centre of the lines of ships. Seeing the flash as *Empire Oak* was hit he called down to *Clonlara's* master and his own (*Alva's*) captain that a new attack on the convoy was being made, but before either master had time to get to the bridge the second of U-564's torpedoes struck *Clonlara*, shattering the starboard side of the ship forward of the bridge and stopping the engines and dynamos.

It was clear at once that *Clonlara* was doomed and Captain Reynolds gave the order to abandon ship. The Eire crew and *Alva* survivors hurried for the boat deck. They were just getting into the boats when another torpedo from U-564 hit the ship in the boiler-room, blowing up the boilers and sending men hurtling through the air into the water.

Speller was helping two men to clear a raft away when this second explosion blew him off the ship. Dazed but otherwise unhurt he saw half a raft rocking in the water, struck out and managed to hang on to it, joined by two other men.

Clonlara's Second Engineer Walker, also blown into the sea by the blast, went under and struggled back to the surface to find himself under the stern of the mangled ship, which had settled by the bow with her propeller out of the water. He swam away as quickly as he could through the debris-strewn sea just as the ship slid down. She had gone within three minutes of the second explosion.

Glimpsing a boat some fifty yards away in the dark, Walker swam on towards it. The boat had been cast off but her intending occupants were scattered by the second explosion, and it had drifted away from the sinking ship. It was half full of water but seemed otherwise little damaged. Walker hauled himself over the side into the pitching boat, afterwards rescuing a swimming donkeyman, and when two other men appeared swimming close by he threw them a lifebuoy and dragged them in too. The boat's oars were firmly lashed down with wire and they had a desperate struggle to free them. Then they were unable to find anything to bale out the water. Walker started to row with one oar, but by now his strength was ebbing, his feet gave way and he could do no more. They drifted helplessly and sodden in the dangerously waterlogged boat.

Fortunately ten minutes later corvette *Campion*, steaming to the rescue, spotted them, but she circled round warily before returning to lower a boat which picked up other survivors from the water while Walker's boat was thrown heaving lines.

At that moment, threshing up out of the dark at menacing speed came the aggressive shape of destroyer *Gurkha*. She had seen a flare and flashing light on the starboard bow and a low, dark object – and turned to ram the suspected U-boat. Coming up at an increasing rate of knots she suddenly sighted *Campion* bows on, saw the red lights of survivors' lifejackets in the water and realised that the suspicious object must be wreckage. Smartly she turned full port wheel and the wreckage and struggling men passed down her starboard side. A few seconds' delay and she would have ploughed straight through them.

Off she went again to port of the convoy, firing starshell, getting contacts one after the other and chasing until the echoes were lost.

Campion carried on with her rescue work. Chief Officer Speller and his two companions had been clinging to their half a raft for nearly an hour before she found them and got them on board. Several of the other men pulled from the water had been injured in the explosion.

The losses from *Clonlara* were heavy. Twelve of the Eire crew, including the master, Captain Reynolds, were killed or missing, while of the *Alva* survivors she had been carrying fourteen were lost, including the master, Captain Palmer.

Meanwhile destroyer *Boreas*, searching the night sea, had obtained a strong U-boat contact, raced after it and fired a six-charge pattern of depth-charges, but without result.

The explosion of the depth-charges was a horrible shock for the survivors of *Empire Oak*, struggling in the water not far away, the sensation being like a heavy kick in the stomach. Grimly, Captain Christian fought to keep afloat. He found himself in company with the chief officer of *Aguila* and his own chief officer. The *Aguila* officer, torpedoed twice in three days, was very despondent and Captain Christian tried to bolster up the man's spirits as they bobbed and floundered in the water. The master found a floating piece of wood which he told the *Aguila* officer to hold on to while he held the other end, so that they should not be separated. His own chief officer kept close to them in the water but he too was very low in spirits, especially when, despite their cries, all remaining ships of the convoy continued on without stopping.

Had they been abandoned?

For two hours the three men fought to stay alive. Captain Christian kept cheering up the other two, sometimes pretending to bully them, so that they would not give up hope, but all were near to exhaustion when corvette *Campanula* finally steamed towards them in the dark. Shouts from the corvette told them to be patient as they could not pick up everyone at once. Captain Christian could see some more bobbing lights at a little distance, and knowing that he and his companions could now hold out for another few minutes but that the others might not be as fortunate, he called out to *Campanula* to carry on.

Campanula lowered a boat to retrieve the other survivors then returned to throw a line to the three men. The light on the *Aguila* officer's lifejacket had gone out so the rope was thrown to Captain Christian. As he tried to catch it he let go of the piece of wood, and with a groan the *Aguila* officer weakly drifted away. With the backlash of the rope Captain Christian lost it, then was suddenly overcome by a terrible cramp in the legs, which left him totally helpless and unable to swim back for the *Aguila* officer. As he beat the water to stay afloat another

Top: The corvette HMS *Campion* whose captain's gallant efforts saved so many lives.

Above: Corvette HMS *Wallflower*, another OG71 escort which was strongly to the rescue.

Above: Coder Walter Wilkinson of HMS *Zinnia*, one of only a handful of survivors.

Right: Commander Charles Cuthbertson, RNR, captain of *Zinnia*, on whom Nicholas Monsarrat modelled his hero for *The Cruel Sea*.

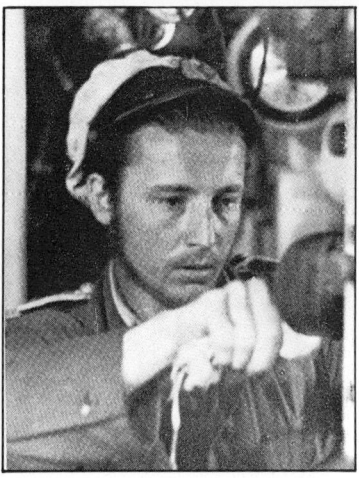

Above Right: Kapitanleutnant Adalbert Schnee of U-201: his torpedoes found *Aguila*.

Above Left: Oberleutnant Reinhard Suhren, whose U-564 brought disaster to *Zinnia*.

rope spun out from the corvette. The exhausted captain grabbed it and called to the corvette crew to haul him in. Once on deck he told them of the plight of the *Aguila* officer and the corvette's boat searched hard for him, but without a light on his lifejacket and no response to their cries it proved impossible to find him.

Meanwhile the captain's own chief officer had also managed to grasp hold of a line and was hauled to safety. Three of the other men rescued by the corvette's boat were injured.

Empire Oak, practically blown out of the water, had suffered great losses. Fourteen of her crew of twenty were killed or drowned. She had also been carrying six survivors from *Aguila* and eleven from *Alva*. Nine of these were lost, including all those from *Aguila*.

It was long after midnight when the last of the *Empire Oak* survivors was rescued and *Campanula* steamed to catch up the other ships. The convoy meanwhile had made its alteration of course as planned to confuse any other night prowlers.

But this time such a ruse was not to succeed. Already Kapitanleutnant Adalbert Schnee's U-201, slayer of *Ciscar* and *Aguila*, had rediscovered the convoy and, despite the efforts of the searching destroyers, was closing in unseen.

6
FLIGHT FROM SLAUGHTER

6

FLIGHT FROM SLAUGHTER

SATURDAY 23 August : 1 a.m. Captain McClean, master of the ss. *Aldergrove*, usually rested about this time, but on this night he decided to stay up on the bridge with his second officer who, after the newest attack on the convoy, seemed to be a bit jittery.

The ship's wireless operator reported to the bridge that he could hear U-boats talking to each other but could not understand what was being said. Captain McClean went to the wireless room and listened in for a few minutes. The wireless continued to pick up transmissions which he could not understand either, and he returned to the bridge.

Minutes afterwards, with the ship keeping strict silence, the puzzled master heard a strange whirring sound at sea and asked his second officer what it was. The officer said he thought it came from a corvette over on the port beam, but then the captain, quickly scanning the dark surface of the sea, glimpsed the white track of a torpedo rushing through the water — it had just missed his ship. Seconds later *Aldergrove* lurched sickeningly as a second torpedo struck the vessel between No.3 hold and the engine-room on the port side. There was a muffled explosion as the torpedo erupted among the cargo of patent fuel, shooting a flood of it into the air with clouds of black smoke. The ship's engines raced for a moment then suddenly stopped.

The captain automatically rang down 'Stop' then tried to

send up emergency rockets, but the firers were damp and would not activate them. So he rushed to give two sets of six short blasts on the ship's whistle to indicate a U-boat on the port side, but when he pulled the whistle lanyard it came adrift in his hands.

The badly-holed ship listed to port and rapidly filled with water. Captain McClean ordered the second officer and the man at the wheel to make ready the boats which were kept griped into the ship's side with patent slips that could be easily knocked away. The starboard boat was lowered first, then the port boat, both being in the water in two minutes, most of the crew stepping into them from the deck, others hastily jumping overboard as the ship, settling quickly under the weight of water, just vanished stern first.

Aldergrove was gone only six minutes after being struck, but even before she sank, the night sea elsewhere shook to a tremendous explosion as another of U-201's torpedoes found its mark. The motorship *Stork*, crammed with cans of petrol, burst violently to the sky in a gigantic sheet of flame, debris flying in all directions and the surface of the sea catching fire all round the vessel. The blaze lit up the scene for miles around, brilliantly illuminating the convoy.

Stork continued to burn fiercely from end to end as *Gurkha* and *Boreas* swept up and down each flank of the convoy with searchlights and firing starshell, but no trace of U-201 or any other U-boat could be found.

Meanwhile, corvette *Campion* worked her way to the weather side of the raging flames and lowered a boat to search for survivors. Its coxswain, Geoff Drummond, a nineteen-year-old leading seaman, took the sixteen-foot dinghy in as close to the burning oil-covered waters as he dared, listening out for whistles and cries, looking for red lights on lifejackets. But they could find only three men, whose survival had been little short of miraculous. They were the *Stork's* second mate and carpenter, who had both escaped from the wrecked bridge, and the second engineer, who had dived out of the porthole from his cabin as it burst into flames, fracturing both his feet in the process. The carpenter, a great burly man, had grabbed his comrades, one under each arm, and pulled them to safety by swimming on his back through a gap in the encircling wall of flaming petrol on the surface. He was such a huge man that the only way he could be hauled into *Campion's* boat was by unshipping the rudder.

There was no further sign of life in the waters surrounding the inferno and the search had to be abandoned. *Stork's* master and eighteen of his crew had perished, either killed in the explosion, burned alive or drowned.

Shortly afterwards the two boats of survivors from ss. *Aldergrove*, who had burned red flares to attract rescuers during an anxious wait of nearly two hours, saw the bows of the searching *Campanula* approaching them slowly through the darkness. As she stopped they pulled alongside and were helped on board, a lengthy and difficult business, as four of them were injured. There were thirty-two men taken from the two boats including the master, Captain McClean, amazingly only one man, a naval gunner, having been lost. The corvette by now resembled a floating ambulance with survivors from *Empire Oak, Alva* and *Aldergrove* on board, several of them badly injured.

Now another merchant ship of the convoy hailed that she had been narrowly missed by a torpedo and destroyer *Boreas* raced off at speed to give chase, firing starshell, but her search too was fruitless.

It seemed ages before the convoy pulled away from sight of the funeral pyre of the luckless *Stork*, her floating remains still ablaze in the distance. The next hour, up to 4 a.m., when the convoy was due to alter course again, was quiet, with no further enemy transmissions being detected by *Gurkha*. But the strain on everyone in the senior destroyer had been heavy. So intense had been her RDF work, the W/T department stretched to capacity, that sending of signals had been kept to a minimum; *Leith*, and even one of the Catalinas, had on occasion been asked to relay a report to Admiralty so as not to interrupt the destroyer's 'tracking'. Now, as *Gurkha's* captain would later frankly admit, after three days almost continuously on the bridge, the reactions of all officers were slower than usual. To think at all had become increasingly difficult. Even the ship's medical officer had been continually assisting with cyphering and plotting and had not been to bed. Towards the end of the night the tensions of the three-day battle were beginning to tell.

On board the corvettes too, weary crews were feeling the strain of being constantly at action-stations. On *Wallflower*, carrying the *Aguila* survivors, men were in two watches, four hours on and four off, which even when uninterrupted had given no one enough sleep, although the captain had bluntly told them repeatedly that two hours was enough for any man. Getting one's head down below decks was, however, a prospect fraught with danger on any of the corvettes; many men slept when they could on mattresses brought from hammocks or bunks on to the upper deck — it felt safer.

It was at this low ebb that the enemy struck again with a devastating blow.

4 a.m. The convoy altered course. As no further attacks had occurred nor any German wireless transmissions been heard, *Gurkha's* tired but watchful captain decided to create a new diversion in order to draw any stalking U-boats away from the convoy. This time, *Gurkha* herself would detach and steam off to provide the 'fireworks'.

After signalling his intention to *Leith*, the signal being picked up by other escorts, Commander Lentaigne sped *Gurkha* on her way at a cracking twenty-seven knots. On reaching a good distance from the convoy he dropped a depth-charge, fired a rocket and afterwards a white Very light followed by a red light, and began a noisy starshell search to the north and north-west.

Unfortunately, at the precise moment that *Gurkha* began her mock battle against an imaginary foe, a very real enemy who had stolen up on the convoy made his deadly thrust.

Oberleutnant Reinhard Suhren, whose earlier victims had been *Empire Oak* and *Clonlara*, had now closed in U-564 on the convoy's port flank. Here, on the port beam, *Wallflower* had been keeping station, but orders came from *Leith* for her to change places with *Zinnia* on the port bow. The two escorts had just effected the change when Suhren loosed his torpedoes.

Zinnia, captained by Lieutenant-Commander Charles Cuthbertson, RNR, kept close station in her new position, carrying out a broad irregular zig-zag at fourteen knots. Both the captain and his No. 1, Lieutenant Harold Chesterman, RNR, were on the bridge. After the grim fate of *Bath* with her exploding depth-charges, Lieutenant-Commander Cuthbertson had ordered all *Zinnia's* depth-charges to be set to safe, and the corvette was keenly on the alert with extra bridge lookouts ordered to keep watch for torpedo tracks.

Lieutenant Chesterman was on the starboard side of the bridge peering through the darkness trying to see the convoy and judge when *Zinnia* was about 2,000 yards off to make a turn to the outward leg. The order 'Port ten' had just been given and the corvette was turning to port and heeling to starboard when a torpedo from U-564 struck her portside abreast of the main bulkhead between the engine-room, bridge and foc'sle.

There was a blinding flash and violent explosion followed by angrily hissing clouds of escaping steam.

The captain had just stepped out of the bridge asdic house. In a split second it collapsed behind him and parts of the ship were thrown into the air – *Zinnia* instantly heeled over on to her starboard beam ends and in five seconds had capsized through 120 degrees, hurling the captain from the compass platform into the water.

So close had he been to the explosion that a mass of flame had singed his hair and eyebrows. Now, dazed but otherwise unhurt, he looked up to see the deck of the ship coming over on top of him as she broke in two around the funnel and a huge swirl of water sucked him down. When he struggled to the surface again his lungs and stomach were filled with oil fuel and he was partially blinded, but he could see the bows rising vertically out of the water – then they disappeared.

HMS *Zinnia*, which had taken seven months and ten days to build, had sunk in fifteen to twenty seconds, leaving hardly a vestige of wreckage.

Commander Cuthbertson struggled in the sea, hampered by the heavy binoculars attached to lanyards round his neck which were nearly strangling him. He tried to blow up his inflatable lifejacket but could not. He heard many cries for help in the water and estimated that there were some forty men floating but he could do nothing to help them. The water was thick with oil fuel and it was all he could do to keep his balance in the swell and his nose and mouth above the oil.

Lieutenant Chesterman had been knocked off his feet by the explosion then washed off the compass platform as it went under. Now he too swam to stay alive in the oil-filled sea.

But it was not the end of *Zinnia's* misery. As she went down, five severe and exceedingly painful underwater explosions shook the men in the water, causing internal injuries to many. Two of the blasts were the result of bulkheads giving way or furnace explosions, but the others were believed to be caused by either depth-charges going off deep when the pistols were forced in by pressure, or enemy torpedoes self-detonating at the end of their run, an appalling and deadly climax to the sinking.

There was confusion among some of the other escorts, who mistook the attack on *Zinnia* for *Gurkha's* pyrotechnic diversion. The captain of the destroyer *Lance*, firmly under this impression, took no action. When the awful realisation of what had really happened dawned on the others a starshell search began, the sight of which puzzled *Gurkha* as she steamed back from her 'battle' to be hailed with the dismaying news.

There followed a long and difficult search for survivors, the men in the water having neither lights nor whistles to indicate their position or anything to support them, for *Zinnia* had gone down so fast there had been no time to cut the lashings on the Carley floats, which sank with the ship.

Campion was once again in the forefront of the search and her gallant captain, Lieutenant-Commander Johnson, RNVR, stopped his ship in the centre of the oil fuel patch – there was no wreckage – and lowered a boat, the boat party under Leading Seaman Drummond urgently probing the sea for a second time in as many hours. The water was covered and stank of the crude oil fuel from *Zinnia's* tanks. It was difficult to get a grip on slippery oil-soaked survivors and haul them into the boat. Three men, gasping for breath with oil clogging their nostrils and eyes, were pulled to safety and taken to *Campion*. Drummond then decided to leave two of his crew of four seamen behind, as with four and himself in the boat they were cramped and restricted as to the numbers they could pick up. Setting out again with his two companions they picked up nine more saturated and exhausted, half-dead men from the filthy, oil-covered sea, several of them injured.

One was young Able Seaman Eric Williams. He had been sleeping with two others on the galley roof on the top deck abaft the funnel when there was a blinding flash, a great 'bump' and he found himself alone in the water, fighting to keep afloat in the oil. He was fortunate to be wearing two lifebelts, one an inflatable-type lifejacket and the other an ordinary naval issue cork belt, which undoubtedly saved him. He was pulled on board *Campion's* boat with hand and eye injuries.

Coder Walter Wilkinson, on being relieved after the middle watch, had gone straight to his action-station as ammunition supply on the upper deck, just astern of the funnel. He was blown into the sea by the explosion and even though his lifejacket was only partially inflated it must have been sufficient to keep him afloat. He saw the bow of *Zinnia* going under, the ship's pennant K98 standing out starkly in the uncertain light. Then came the severe underwater explosions. Wilkinson found himself in a group of half a dozen men all shouting for help from time to time in between swallowing fuel oil and other filth. He paddled with his left arm to keep afloat as his right arm would not function, and his right eye was closed from a wound above it. He could do nothing but just keep going, weakening by the minute, hoping against hope for some means of rescue, struggling on as at least two men near him gave up and slipped under. He was almost done when *Campion's* boat found him, too far gone to protest when he was pulled inboard by someone grabbing his sorely wounded arm.

Of two others found in the water one man was unconscious, being protectively supported by his companion. It must have taken considerable effort, for the unconscious man was tall and heavily built, but his companion insisted that his friend be taken into the boat first, and when he himself was hoisted into the boat he tenderly nursed his friend, a stoker, until they were both helped on board *Campion*.

Another man pulled from the oil was a fortunate seaman who had been in the crow's nest when *Zinnia* was hit. As she went down he had practically stepped into the sea.

Zinnia's captain, Lieutenant-Commander Cuthbertson, had struggled for forty minutes to keep afloat before finding the trunk of a body which had been blasted and was buoyant; he clutched on to this to keep himself alive. He had been in the water for over an hour when he heard the throb, throb, throb of the propeller of a searching corvette as she passed through the oil fuel patch. It was HMS *Campanula*, but as he sighted her through oil-dimmed eyes to his astonishment and dismay she steamed past him at half a cable's distance . . . convincing him that he had been left to die. It was ages before *Campion's* dinghy then came upon him, still clinging to the buoyant corpse of one of his crew, near complete exhaustion and ready to meet his Maker. As hands hauled him inboard he was dimly aware of the exclamation of a Cockney sailor: 'Blimey, he must be an orficer, he's got a pair of glasses round his bleedin' neck!'

The captain's No. 1, Lieutenant Chesterman, had also known black despair before *Campion's* boat finally found him. After swimming for a long time Chesterman eventually found one of *Zinnia's* smoke-floats to which he clung tenaciously, cutting his fingers and bruising his chest on the igniter. But as time elapsed his will to survive drained away. He gave up, arguing with himself that there was no point in prolonging the agony; there had been no time to send up a distress flare or transmit a wireless signal so nobody knew they had been sunk, the situation seemed hopeless. He relaxed his hold . . .

He was a few feet down when a vision of his wife, Caroline, and what life could hold for him (he was only twenty-four) came vividly to mind. It spurred him to fight back; he determined to regain the smoke-float and cling on to it till it sank. But how long would it support him? As he clung on he tried to recall for how long such things floated. Each smoke-float had a soluble plug in its buoyancy chamber so that after doing its job of emitting smoke it would sink, but he could not remember if the time the plug took to dissolve was twenty minutes, forty minutes or an hour.

And that was how *Campion's* boat found him. Mercifully the plug held out and he was still clinging on when he spotted the dark shape of the dinghy. He started to yell — loudly and strongly, he thought — but he was pitifully weak; in the boat someone thought they heard a croak from the water and they turned to investigate. Chesterman parted from his life-saving float and was hauled in.

Campion's boat saved twelve survivors in all.

Zinnia's captain had just sufficient strength left in him to climb up the ladder but once aboard the corvette could only crawl on all fours along the deck, now completely blinded by oil fuel and unable to stop shaking with cold. Meanwhile his No. 1, having been carried to the wardroom, valiantly told his bearers that he was all right so they let him go, whereupon he collapsed and pitched heavily on to the second engineer of *Stork* who was sitting on the deck with legs outstretched, both feet fractured from his dive out of the porthole. The engineer never uttered one word of protest. Chesterman gave himself up to vomiting oil fuel and blood; meantime his captain had collapsed in the officers' heads with blood and oil fuel coming out of him at both ends.

The corvette's crew, led by SBA Thompson, showed great care and efficiency in their treatment of *Zinnia's* exhausted and injured men, rubbing them down with cotton waste, removing oil from their bodies with paraffin and from their eyes with petrol, the burly ship's carpenter survivor from *Stork* proving a cheerful tower of strength in helping with the first-aid work, the bandaging and improvising splints for fractured limbs. He bathed *Zinnia's* captain in paraffin, cleaned his face with petrol, wrapped him in a blanket and put him on the floor in the first lieutenant's cabin. Cuthbertson felt something was wrong and found that a silver compact and chain were missing from around his neck. In the compact, which bore his name and official number, was a caul, a sailor's most precious possession: with a caul on his person he would never drown. Cuthbertson's wife was born with one and it had been presented to him by his mother-in-law. It undoubtedly seemed to have saved him this day. It was while searching for the compact, which he thankfully found stowed up aloft on a beam, that he came upon his No. 1, Harold Chesterman, looking pretty terrible but still alive and kicking after being similarly cleaned up by *Stork's* resourceful carpenter, who then found both men some gear to wear.

Injured Coder Wilkinson found himself placed on a bunk with someone forcing him to smoke a cigarette to make him sick in order to bring up the oil fuel he had swallowed. He refused instinctively as he did not smoke, not realising it was for his own good; doing the same with attempts to get him to pass water.

Even in their distress some men found humour, not least the survivor from the crow's nest, a Regular seaman, who patted his oil-tortured stomach with relish. In his mess, he said, they had just about come to the end of the line with their ration of potatoes and had had to make a solemn decision whether to have a good share of potatoes with their 'pot mess' that night or have only a small portion, keeping the remainder for the following day. They had finally voted, 'Let's have all the spuds tonight — we may not be here tomorrow'; so he was happy to have had something like a full meal before being torpedoed.

Meantime the searching *Wallflower* had found three other struggling members of *Zinnia's* crew, one a young Newfoundlander. While in the water he had swallowed an enormous amount of oil fuel and was violently sick. Afterwards he could not be persuaded to go below but remained on deck staring at the water, very badly shocked. At the same time *Campanula*, whose company included Lieutenant Nicholas Monsarrat, RNVR, had found two other oil-saturated survivors, one of them a badly injured sub-lieutenant, and pulled them in. But that made only seventeen survivors in all . . . it had been a dreadful disaster.

But all was not over yet.

Destroyer *Boreas*, sighting some fourteen miles from the convoy the flash of gunfire and trails of tracer bullets, followed by the bursting incandescence of a burning ship, steamed off at twenty-five knots to investigate.

She found the Norwegian coal and coke ship ss. *Spind* in a sorry plight. *Spind* had missed the convoy's alteration of course, steamed on alone and become prey to a surfaced U-boat which raked her with heavy gunfire. *Spind's* own gun crew got off only two shells in reply before her company were forced to scatter to the boats with the vessel strongly ablaze amidships. The second mate was shot and injured by machine-gun bullets from the U-boat while lowering one of the boats, the German afterwards making off at speed convinced that the ship was doomed.

Boreas arrived and closed on the burning *Spind* to find the wounded mate hanging on a lifeline from the ship's davit head. *Boreas* lowered a boat with orders to rescue him, assess the damage to the ship and examine the possibilities of salvaging her — a dangerous mission with *Spind's* ready-use ammunition and PAC rockets exploding in all directions in the fire.

Suddenly the destroyer thought she got a U-boat contact on her asdic at which she fired off a single depth-charge. She could not fire more because of the proximity of the survivors' boats and her own boat. It was thought at first that the U-boat had submerged and was hiding under, or nearly under, the burning *Spind*, but later it seemed more probable that it was not a U-boat at all, the echo really coming from *Spind* herself.

Boreas now took *Spind's* two boatloads of survivors safely on board, a lengthy job. *Campanula*, which had arrived to help, also got a believed U-boat contact close by and, the survivors cleared, fired a full pattern of charges, but the enemy, if it was him, had slipped away.

As the early light of dawn streaked the sky it became clear that the *Spind*, her forehold still well afire, was slowly sinking and quite impossible to salvage. She was a hazard and it was decided to speed her demise. After a salvo from *Boreas* the luckless vessel slipped below the surface in a last surge of flames and scalding steam.

As the various incomplete reports came in to *Gurkha* the events of the long night were pieced together, though as yet without any clear idea of the death toll. Five merchant ships and one escort vessel sunk. *Gurkha's* signal to Admiralty reporting the losses made sorry reading.

On board *Campion*, Lieutenant-Commander Cuthbertson, ill as he was, performed a final sad duty. *Campion* had picked up several bodies from *Zinnia* as well as the survivors and he now read from the Naval Prayer Book as they were committed to the deep.

The depleted convoy ploughed on. During the morning another destroyer, HMS *Vidette*, joined, and *Gurkha* re-adjusted the screening positions of the escorts for OG71's remaining fourteen merchant ships. *Campion* asked for *Gurkha's* medical officer to help with her injured survivors from *Zinnia* and *Stork*, and he was transferred with *Leith* screening, but the doctor could not save the badly wounded stoker from *Zinnia* whose friend had tried so desperately to keep him alive. He died and was buried at sea.

Gurkha now began to pick up more enemy transmissions, from which it was evident that the U-boats were reporting their successful attack. The destroyer also investigated several more suspected U-boat contacts, but still without result. And time was running out, for her fuel now was at a critical level, as was that of *Lance*. The pair of them simply could not stay with the convoy any longer.

At midday *Gurkha* handed over leadership of the outer escort to destroyer *Wivern* and steamed off with *Lance* for Gibraltar, where they would arrive the following day, *Gurkha* with only three per cent of fuel remaining.

But there was no question of OG71 following on after them to Gibraltar. Everything pointed to the U-boat wolf pack being still at large and regrouping. If the convoy continued on course, drawing nearer to the coast on its slow, curving path in towards Gibraltar, further determined attacks were inevitable and it was clear that the weary escorts just could not cope. The merchant ships simply could not risk a further night at sea. The grave situation had been discussed by *Gurkha* and *Leith*, and in the early afternoon an Admiralty signal arrived giving the firm order: 'All ships of OG71 are to be escorted to Tagus and instructed to proceed to Lisbon . . .'

Accordingly the whole convoy, not only those ships actually bound for Lisbon, turned and made directly for the Portuguese coast, where they could expect to enter the River Tagus and reach the safe neutral port of Lisbon before dusk. Once there, most of the escorts would detach and steam on for Gibraltar, leaving the convoy to await the arrival of fresh escorts to take it on its last lap to the Rock.

It was a chastening and highly distasteful decision to have to make but, in the circumstances, the only sensible one. Nevertheless there were angry men in the naval ships who felt thoroughly sick at having to turn tail and flee the scene; none more so than *Campanula's* Lieutenant Monsarrat, who, in the post-war years, would make such an impact as a sea-war novelist. It was, he termed it, 'as bitter an act of surrender as could ever come our way.'

The Admiralty meanwhile, upon receiving *Gurkha's* earlier

report of the final night's tragedies, had immediately sent the following terse signal to the Flag Officer Commanding North Atlantic, in Gibraltar:

'The fact that no contacts with U-boats were made during these three night attacks is disturbing. On arrival of escorts request you will interview commanding officers and report whether there were any new or special circumstances which may account for this.'

Top: Zinnia's Lieutenant-Commander Cuthbertson on the bridge in khaki battle rig with *(left)* his No. 1, Lieutenant Harold Chesterman, RNR.
Left: Pre-*Zinnia* days: Lieutenant Chesterman in bitter seas on Northern Patrol.
Above Right: Nicholas Monsarrat, who was a lieutenant in the corvette HMS *Campanula*. Convoy OG71 was his enduring nightmare, his worst experience of the war.

The boat from HMS *Campion* which searched the dark, oil covered sea for survivors of *Zinnia*.

Above: Telegraphist Tom Shuttleworth of HMS *Wallflower* who drew the chapter-head drawings and painted the cover for this book.
Right: Leading Seaman Geoff Drummond who led the boat party.

7
MISSING, PRESUMED DROWNED

7

MISSING, PRESUMED DROWNED

A SIGNAL from corvette HMS *Wallflower* as she steamed on her way to Gibraltar, giving her estimated time of arrival, told the miserable story of OG71:

'To FOCNA: ETA 1600 August 24th. HMS *Campion* in company. Request ambulance for 6 seriously injured from *Campion* and 2 seriously injured from *Wallflower*. Have on board master and 5 merchant seamen 2 naval ratings (passengers) 1 naval rating (Commodore's staff) all from *Aguila*, 3 ratings HMS *Zinnia*. *Campion* has on board C.O., 1st lt., 9 ratings from *Zinnia*, 8 from *Clonlara*, 4 from *Alva*, 3 from *Stork*.'

Two hours after the arrival of *Wallflower* and *Campion* at Gibraltar, HMS *Campanula* steamed in with yet more injured men among her survivors from *Empire Oak*, *Alva*, *Aldergrove* and *Zinnia*.

The ambulances were even busier that Sunday evening than they had been two days earlier, when HMS *Hydrangea* had arrived signalling for help for six seriously injured and two other cot cases, her survivors from *Bath*, whom, thankfully, she had brought in without a further death.

The wounded survivors landed on stretchers from the three newly-arrived corvettes were speedily taken to hospital. Men with lesser injuries — the 'walking wounded' — queued for treatment.

The exhausted crews of the corvettes thankfully sought food and sleep. As on *Wallflower*, where a sentry was sent down from the base to guard the gangway and the whole ship 'piped down'. Men found it difficult to close their eyes for a time, they were so sore through lack of sleep.

For the non-hospital cases among the raggle-taggle clad merchant seamen survivors, just sick and weary sailors looking forward to a good meal and a bed, there was a shock. On being landed from the corvettes they were shepherded together by an official of the Ministry of War Transport who then led them to the shipping office, some having to walk through the streets barefoot. There, after a frustrating, hungry wait of several hours it was finally arranged for some to go to the Sailors' Home and some to the Victoria Hotel. The man from the Ministry explained that he had no funds at his disposal and could do nothing else for them: no loan of money, no clothes, not even a pair of boots for bruised bare feet.

The merchant captains among the survivors were almost as badly off and did not mince words when they came to write their official reports.

'The accommodation and food at the Victoria Hotel was very bad. The wash basin in my room was filthy and there was no soap. After spending twenty minutes clearing the basin, the water stopped running. We complained about the poor accommodation and were later found rooms in the Grand Hotel, where we were able at least to get a salt water bath. The food here was also very poor . . .'

'We were sent to the Victoria Hotel which was a filthy place and the food very bad. The wash basins and everything about the place were dirty and we had to go out into the town and buy our own soap, and even had to carry our own water to our bedrooms. I consider that our reception and treatment while at Gibraltar left very much to be desired . . .'

'We were put in at the Grand Hotel, which was terribly dirty and really rather awful, but it was the only place available, RN personnel also being accommodated there. I understand that they (the Ministry) are trying to acquire a big house for survivors, or failing this a ship in the harbour, as they have large numbers of shipwrecked people at times . . .'

And one master cuttingly observed:

'The man at the Ministry stated that he had no funds at his

disposal, but I noticed in the local Gazette that £250 had just been subscribed for a fund for Distressed Merchant Seamen, to enable them to buy necessary clothing. There were about 134 survivors at Gibraltar and clothing was costly and very scarce . . .'

It was a disquieting if not disgraceful state of affairs that had men who asked for little being given less than nothing; men who bravely risked a dangerous sea as a matter of course being reduced to carping about bad food and filthy wash basins.

There was no complete picture of the convoy's losses. Men only knew their own part in it together with scraps of information and rumours heard about other ships sunk and human casualties.

'Have the Wrens arrived?' was the eager question persistently asked of members of the naval crews. Gibraltar had been looking forward so long to their coming. But it was a question none could answer.

What *had* happened to the *Aguila* Wrens? Nothing was clear, though stories began to circulate of some of the girls having been picked up, including a few who were said to have been saved by *Empire Oak*, only to be lost when the tug was torpedoed. In the general security clamp-down at Gibraltar it was not even known how many Wrens *Aguila* had been carrying; some thought as many as fifty.

Apart from speculation about the sad fate of the girls, what affected the naval men most was the appalling loss of HMS *Zinnia*. The escort corvettes, officers and crews, worked in close company, which made the loss all the greater; but there was little time to dwell on the incident for the remaining corvettes were quickly at sea again on a U-boat sweep, though not before the forlorn figure of *Zinnia's* captain had visited *Campanula*.

To *Campanula's* Lieutenant Nicholas Monsarrat, RNVR, *Zinnia's* Lieutenant-Commander Charles Cuthbertson had been a man apart. RNVR officers, sarcastically dubbed 'weekend yachtsmen', often had to put up with rough if not downright unpleasant treatment from RN and RNR officers, the professionals. Monsarrat had found his own tough RNR captain to be no exception, 'surly and ungenerous' to pink-cheeked amateurs like himself, although a superb ship-handler. But Cuthbertson, whom Monsarrat had met several times with the corvettes working so closely together, was different.

Friendly and extremely capable, Cuthbertson had come straight into the war from the Union Castle Mail Steamship Company. The son of an RN captain, he had joined the Royal Naval Reserve at the early age of sixteen, and with Union Castle had gained his master's ticket at twenty-four. Still only in his mid-thirties he had been fighting the sea war since the first week of hostilities. Early duties had seen him in command of anti-submarine trawlers and on extra hazardous service in the Norwegian campaign commanding the 'Gubbins Flotilla', five ancient Aberdeen drifters laden down with Tommy-guns, explosives of all types, camouflage nets and warm clothing for Major-General Gubbins and his troops somewhere in Norway behind the enemy lines; Cuthbertson delivered the goods close to the general's hideout, in spite of being sunk twice by enemy action. Before *Zinnia*, he had commanded the corvette *Hibiscus* and won the DSC for his ship spiritedly attacking a U-boat unsupported.

Although Cuthbertson was only four years older than Monsarrat there was an ocean of experience between them. But Monsarrat had been drawn to the man by his friendliness and calm, steady nature, so unlike the crude attitude of others, and he felt it keenly as the torpedoed captain came on board *Campanula* tired and drained, 'an oily, half-dead master mariner.'

Cuthbertson was still suffering so badly from oil fuel poisoning that the only thing he could keep down in his stomach was a gin and tonic, for the offer of which he was grateful, though he was somewhat bemused when Monsarrat impetuously pulled out paper and pencil and started peppering him with questions . . . 'Tell me, what was your reaction when you realised you had been torpedoed?' . . . 'What were your thoughts when you were swimming in the water?' . . . and many others, making quick note of his replies.

Whatever notes Monsarrat, the novelist, took down at the time he would save for his fiction. But he did describe that meeting in a telling paragraph in his autobiography, years afterwards.

> 'He (Cuthbertson) had nothing much to say except thank you: what man could have had anything to say, who had just lost seventy-five of his crew and a corvette which, turning under full helm, was hit below the boiler-room and broke in half while those left alive on the upper deck were still shocked and staring?' (*Life Is A Four Letter Word*; Cassell)

Cuthbertson had refused to go to hospital for treatment. Next day he flew by Catalina back to the UK to report to the Director of Anti-Submarine Warfare and the head of the Casualty Division. Then, from his home in Dorset, still a sick man, he composed his secret report for the Admiralty on the loss of his ship.

With the departure to the UK of *Zinnia's* captain, Lieutenant Chesterman was left to look after the sunken corvette's survivors and get them home as best he could. Half of them had gone to hospital, the others to a rest camp. The No. 1 found himself in a tough position with no ship, no papers and no paybooks. No one wanted to know them, to supply clothing, toiletries or cash, except their own Escort Group, who did what they could. The Transport people told him that he and his men would just have to join the long line of survivors and other unfortunates trying to get home.

Sadly, among the small number of *Zinnia* survivors death struck again when a young sub-lieutenant, one of the only two men saved by *Campanula*, died in hospital despite having two blood transfusions.

Lieutenant Chesterman was grateful to the cruiser HMS *Manchester* for offering to conduct the burial of the young officer. *Manchester* was, in fact, repaying a debt. On *Zinnia's* last visit to Gibraltar before OG71, the *Manchester* had come in from a Malta convoy with more than a dozen men dead after she was struck by a torpedo which had hit a fuel tank, fractured the bulkhead between the tank and the W/T office and tragically drowned the occupants in fuel oil. Their bodies could not be recovered until the ship had dry-docked and the oil been drained out, but because the sailors died at sea they were to be buried at sea, and *Zinnia* was detailed to do the grim job. No canvas was to be had in Gibraltar at that time so the oil-soaked bodies were sewn up in blankets. As the bodies were not weighted, after the burial ceremony they all floated to the surface of the sea. In a sad situation *Zinnia's* captain decided to give them a Viking's funeral by going to action-stations and opening fire. The stench of death had not really left *Zinnia* until she herself was sunk.

Now, *Zinnia's* sub-lieutenant was buried in the military section of the North Front Cemetery with seamen and Marines from HMS *Manchester* carrying out the service. All the *Zinnia* survivors were present.

The only survivors of OG71 to land at Lisbon, instead of being brought on to Gibraltar later, were the master and twenty-four of the crew of the sunken Vice-Commodore ship *Ciscar*. Their reception even in this brightly-lit neutral port was not without its frustrations. They arrived independently of the rest of the convoy in their rescuing vessel, the ss. *Petrel*, on the Saturday evening. The captain of the *Petrel* went ashore on Sunday morning taking a list of the survivors he was carrying, but there were talks, papers to settle and interminable things to sign, so that it was Monday afternoon before any of the *Ciscar* men were finally allowed ashore after a 'lost' forty-eight hours. They had no money, no belongings, and no clothes except those they had been able to borrow from the crew of the *Petrel*.

But the surprise arrival of a British convoy, or the remains of it, off spy-ridden Lisbon had been of considerable interest. In this neutral port there was no security blanket as in Gibraltar; the news was anyone's if it could be got at, and the coming ashore of the survivors from *Ciscar* was a godsend to newspaper reporters and spies alike. The survivors were immediately pursued for their stories. The result was a colourful despatch to the *Daily Telegraph* in London by that paper's 'special correspondent' which turned the convoy's ignominious defeat into a near victory, the probable reason for the Ministry of Information censors in London allowing it to be printed. The report appeared on 26 August 1941 under the headlines: 14 SHIPS BEAT U-BOATS AND PLANES: RUNNING FIGHT OFF FRENCH COAST: FALSE GERMAN CLAIMS. It began:

> 'After facing repeated bombing and submarine attacks fourteen ships of a British convoy of twenty-one arrived in Lisbon to prove the falsity of German claims, for all of them were sunk by the Berlin radio, together with a destroyer, a corvette and another escort vessel.
>
> 'Actually only six vessels and the ocean-going tug *Empire Oak* were sunk . . . There is no truth in the Nazi claim to have sunk a destroyer and an escort vessel.'

The report went on to give a brief day-by-day description of enemy attacks on the convoy which, it said, had left England for Gibraltar on 12 August. Understandably, perhaps, in the anxiety to get a good story most of the facts were wrong, including the information that a corvette was torpedoed 'but there is no confirmation that she was sunk,' and, 'It is believed that the majority of the crews of the torpedoed vessels were picked up by other ships.'

The report quoted 'the captain of one of the merchant vessels' whose apparent statements, though making brave reading, were somewhat wide of the truth. But the informant did praise a Catalina which 'did magnificent work in protecting the convoy', and the 'strong naval escort which dropped many depth-charges', adding, 'I cannot say for certain, but I have a strong feeling that the German submarine fleet is now fewer by two or three U-boats.'

Stirring stuff. The report accurately named all but three of the merchant ships to arrive off Lisbon; but, except for the reference to *Empire Oak*, there was no mention of those lost. A similar report from Reuters was allowed to appear in other daily newspapers the same day describing the convoy's 'exciting escape' to the Tagus, with another unidentified merchant captain emphasising that it was his sixteenth convoy along the same route and the very first one in which a ship had been lost.

Unfortunately the 'false claims' of the Germans were quickly proved to be not so false next day, though there was carefully nothing to link the following brief official communiqué with the Gibraltar convoy:

'The former United States destroyer *Bath*, manned by the Royal Norwegian Navy, has been sunk. All possible steps are being taken to advise the next-of-kin of those lost, said Admiral Diesen, C-in-C of the Royal Norwegian Navy yesterday. This is the first of the former American destroyers to be sunk in the Allies' service. The First Lord of the Admiralty, Mr Alexander, has sent a message of sympathy to the Norwegian Minister of Defence, Col. Ljunberg.'

No mention of casualties. In fact, when the final count was made, *Bath* had lost a grim total of eighty-three officers and men, thirteen of them British.

In the *Daily Telegraph* another paragraph tucked away elsewhere in the same issue reported:

'It was officially confirmed yesterday that, as stated in the *Daily Telegraph*, six merchant vessels and one tug were sunk in the recent attack on a British convoy off Spain. The names are given as *Stork*, *Ciscar*, *Algia*, *Clonlara*, *Spind*, *Aguila* and *Empire Oak*, with a total tonnage of 11,094.'

One ship misspelt and another omitted, for in fact eight vessels had been sunk.

But the names of ships given meant little except to relatives of the crews — if they saw them, and if they knew the vessels their menfolk were on. And even though *Aguila* was named, no one was to know of her role as Commodore ship or the large number of passengers she was carrying; the immense hush-hush which prevailed over this period of the war prevented both the Press and near relatives from obtaining details of ships, crews, and the drafts they carried.

No proper report of the convoy was given then or later, and no casualty list. Nor was there the smallest reference to the convoy or even to its role at sea when an announcement of the death of Vice-Admiral Patrick Parker appeared in *The Times*; it merely stated that he had been 'killed on active service'.

And the Wrens?

On a number of days during September several unrelated paragraphs like these appeared in the newspapers:

'Two Wren casualties announced yesterday were 3rd Officer Margaret Eulalie Chappé Hall, only daughter of the late Rev. John Chappé Hall, Bucks Green, on active service, and 3rd Officer Cecelia Mary Blake Forster, daughter of the late Major and Mrs A.B. Blake Forster, missing presumed drowned.' And:

'The eighth Wren to be named as a casualty this week is 3rd Officer Kathleen Miller, daughter of Mrs J.A. Miller and the late Mr Henry Miller, Aberystwyth. She is reported missing, presumed lost at sea.'

Missing, presumed drowned, and not a mention of why or where. In death the *Aguila's* happy band of Wrens had been parted, just casualties to be reported here and there on different days.

Winifred Shand, skipper of the Leith Sea Rangers, had worried about the last letter she received from young Madge Barnes, written before setting sail for Gibraltar:

'. . . If anything should happen to me. Skipper. I want you to know that the happiest moments of my life were when I was at a Sea Rangers muster . . .'

It was far too ominous, not a bit like bubbly Madge. Winifred wrote off straight away by air mail to the address in Gibraltar which Madge had given her, so that Chief Wren Barnes would have a friendly letter waiting for her when she arrived.

A few days later Captain Smith, the Sea Rangers' instructor, who was working with shipping in Leith, rang Skipper Shand to say he was very worried as information had come his way that a convoy had been attacked. He would let her know if he had any further word. Hours later he rang again to tell her that the ship carrying the Wrens to Gibraltar had been lost with none of the girls being saved. It was a dreadful shock for them both. Winifred went out at once to see Madge's mother . . . 'She was terribly brave and said she knew that was the way Madge would have liked to have died. I went and saw her as often as I could . . .'

Mrs Vera Laughton Mathews, Director of the WRNS, was driving along the south-west coast, inspecting Wren bases, when she received the news from the Admiralty of the shattering blow her Service had suffered. All her girls wiped out as one. It was both a cruel, unbelievable tragedy and a deep personal loss, for she had known every girl, picked every one, the cream of her flock. Her own grief would equal that of the parents and next-of-kin to whom, as head of the Service, she would write a personal message of sympathy and condolence.

At this trying time, to their credit, those in high places who, at best, had been somewhat diffident to her efforts were moved to realise the extent of the loss and the consternation it brought not only in the WRNS but throughout the Navy. The First Lord sent a personal note of sympathy, as did other members of the Board of Admiralty.

'We were not then enured to tragedy — later losses (and there were many) came as a less personal shock,' Mrs Laughton Mathews would recall. 'These were the pioneers. And I think their death brought home to many for the first time, a realisation of the quality of Service women, their courage, their earnestness — that young women were not joining up to wear a smart uniform or to have a good time, that they accepted willingly a share in the hardship, the responsibility, and the perils of Service life.'

None would ever forget the horror and distress felt by all when news of the disaster filtered through to the ranks of the WRNS. Nor the brave and inspiring sequel. Gibraltar had been anxiously awaiting the lost Wrens, and in response to a further urgent signal from the Rock a second draft of girls was hastily got together. In spite of the fate of their comrades, volunteers were immediately forthcoming, more than two hundred of them. This time there was no opportunity for prolonged selection, the new draft was chosen, kitted out and packed off just as soon as possible.

But there was one very important difference. As a direct result of the *Aguila* tragedy, the Admiralty's archaic rule that women must not travel in warships was scrapped overnight. The new draft of Wrens took passage to Gibraltar in a destroyer, actually carrying out some watch duties on board during the voyage.

And in future WRNS personnel, commissioned or otherwise, would always be granted passage in His Majesty's warships whenever possible.

Meanwhile, in Gibraltar the stranded naval survivors of HMS *Zinnia*, led by their first lieutenant, had sought to get home.

One morning in the Admiral's office, dressed in borrowed and ill-fitting shirt and shorts, capless and with no insignia, and shod in carpet slippers, Lieutenant Chesterman was bawled out by the chief-of-staff. But on being told that the No. 1 was dressed as he was because it was the best he could scrounge, the face of authority changed completely, took Chesterman into his inner sanctum and listened to his tale of woe. Told that other ships of the Escort Group were willing to take the No. 1's men but that his efforts to arrange this were being frustrated by Transport Control, the chief-of-staff ordered Chesterman to make whatever arrangements he thought best and send out the necessary signals in his exalted name. Chesterman did so in quick time, collected all his men who were fit to leave and got them on board ships of the Group. He himself joined *Campion*, the ship that had rescued them, sharing the night watches with her captain on the run home.

(Lieutenant Harold Chesterman later rejoined Lieutenant-Commander Cuthbertson as his No. 1 when Cuthbertson took command of the newly-built corvette HMS *Snowflake*. When, after some months, Cuthbertson moved on to command the destroyer HMS *Scimitar* he made special recommendation to the Commodore of Western Approaches that Chesterman take over his old ship (something that happened very rarely, first lieutenants usually moving to a different vessel to take command): and so Chesterman, as captain of *Snowflake*, became at the time the youngest officer to command a major war vessel).

One *Zinnia* survivor obliged to remain behind at Gibraltar for a time was Coder Walter Wilkinson, suffering from his badly injured arm.

As with all naval wounded the cause and details of Wilkinson's injuries were officially entered on Form M.183, the parchment 'Certificate for Wounds and Hurts', together with a brief personal description and the requisite answer to the solemn question under King's Regulations as to whether he was 'Sober' or 'Not sober' at the time (wryly testified to by Lieutenant Chesterman).

Wilkinson was many weeks in the Army 65th general hospital. He underwent surgery but the wounds would not heal, and in November he was shipped home in the cruiser HMS *Edinburgh* along with other walking wounded. He had no kit but the Gibraltar stores had no warm clothes to issue. On board *Edinburgh* he and his companions had to sleep in any corner they could find as the sick bay was full, and they messed anywhere there was room. Landed at Greenock and taken to hospital near Glasgow, Wilkinson was eventually taken south to the naval hospital at Chatham, where he endured a long series of operations, bone being taken from his leg to build up his arm. It would be eighteen months before he recovered sufficiently to be fit for light duty.

On the merchant seamen side, another man subjected to a long stay in hospital at Gibraltar was David Kerr, the young steward on *Aguila* who had been blown out of the ship in the double explosion. With a compound fracture of the right leg, left leg also broken, spine and jaw fractured, teeth broken and chipped, Kerr's recovery would also be a slow process, having to spend many long months in hospital in the UK to repair the injuries, the effects of which would remain with him for the rest of his life.

8
WHY DID IT HAPPEN?

Launching the memorial lifeboat *Aguila Wren* at Aberystwyth in the summer of 1952.

Top: Dedication of the seat on the Lighthouse Pier at Scarborough in 1972 in memory of the lost Wrens of the *Aguila*.
Above Right: Survivors today: Captain Charles Cuthbertson, DSC, RD, RNR (ret.) and ex-Coder Walter Wilkinson of HMS *Zinnia* at a reunion of the Flower Class Corvette Association.
Top Left: Ex-leading Seaman Geoff Drummond who saved both men above; and two survivors of *Aguila*: *Centre Left:* ex-Yeoman of Signals Fred Buckingham.
Bottom Left: ex-LAM William Churchouse of the Fleet Air Arm.

8

WHY DID IT HAPPEN?

WHAT had gone wrong on the fateful voyage of convoy OG71?

The 'inquest', conducted entirely in secret, was a lengthy affair, from interrogation of commanding officers of the naval escorts to examination of survivors' reports, studies by naval analysts and deliberation at the highest level at the Admiralty.

Why had a routine convoy, adequately escorted, lost eight merchant ships, plus two warships, with the loss of nearly 400 lives, and been forced to give up, turn tail and flee to the safety of a neutral port? This after the previous convoy had not lost a ship.

The Flag Officer Commanding North Atlantic, who had been directed by the Admiralty to question the escort commanders, reported that:

> 'Apparently undue reliance on RDF by *Gurkha* led him to take the destroyers out unduly for an offensive sweep and they were still remote from the convoy when the first attack developed.
>
> 'The port flank and quarter of the convoy were inadequately guarded from the direction of the third attack, the close screen having dropped back to pick up survivors from the second attack and a destroyer of outward screen detached to create a diversion.

'No illumination was provided by the close screen on the flanks of the convoy during any attack.'

But after these observations on the conduct of the escorts both FOCNA and his captain of destroyers were strongly critical of the convoy's alteration of route. FOCNA put it to the Admiralty as bluntly as he could:

'Though unaware of their nature I presume that good reasons existed to necessitate the re-routing of the convoy within such easy reconnaissance range of enemy shore-based aircraft. It appears abundantly clear that U-boats were homed on to OG71 by aircraft and unless there are strong reasons for doing so I am very averse to convoys in the North Atlantic Command being routed within easy range of enemy aircraft especially if beyond effective range of our own.'

The Commander-in-Chief Western Approaches (Admiral Noble) took note of FOCNA's remarks. The convoy's route had been shortened principally because of the believed limited fuel capacity of ships in convoy, but if ships' fuel capacity allowed, convoys could make a wider sweep.

He pronounced that the destroyers with the convoy should not have been used as a striking force or left the convoy to conduct an offensive sweep. Furthermore, two groups of escorts under divided control was unsatisfactory, particularly with the corvettes being inexperienced at working as a team; it was essential that all escorts should act under one senior officer. However, he disagreed that the captain of *Gurkha* had placed too much reliance on RDF, which had proved its certain use, and declared that Commander Lentaigne had 'shown enterprise and initiative under trying circumstances'.

The vexing arguments over why none of the escorts had actually encountered, much less destroyed, a U-boat, taxed the naval strategists, who went over the warships' movements in critical detail, studying the plots of commanders, but the simple truth as it finally emerged was inescapable. The convoy had been beaten by the enemy's superior tactics.

It had been OG71's misfortune to encounter a full and very successful attack by German planes and U-boats working together. In the past, the long-range Focke-Wulf Condors – the four-engined plane that Churchill called 'the scourge of the Atlantic' – had individually bombed and shot to pieces Allied ships. Some earlier attempts had been made by the Germans to

99

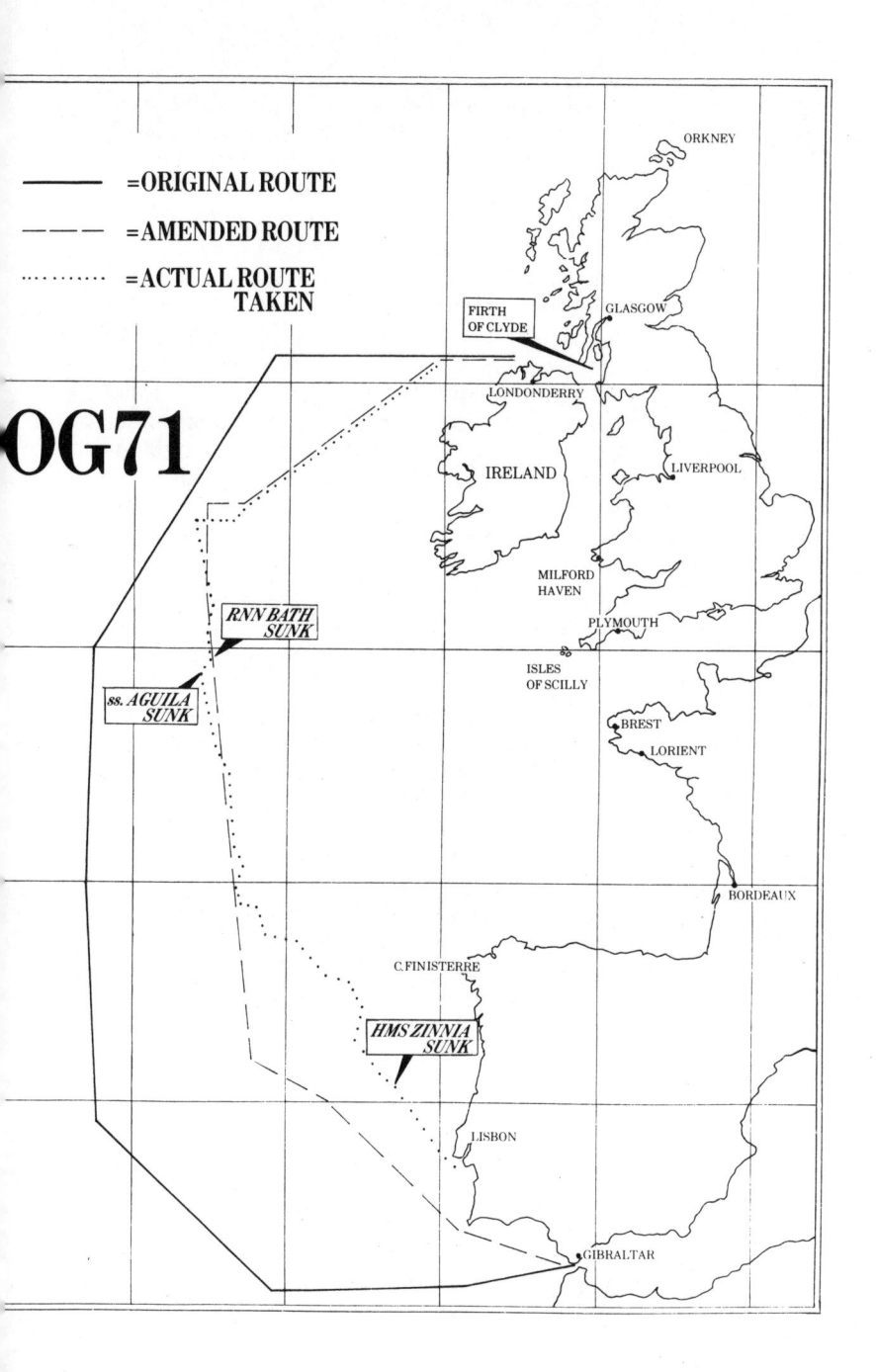

have their planes and U-boats acting in unison, but never very satisfactorily. Now, however, with improved wireless facilities, this tactic had been perfected, the Condors acting as shadowers to home-in the wolf pack with alarming results.

In fact the convoy was doomed from the moment that the first Focke-Wulf of enemy group 1-KG-40 flew over and reported its position. Later that same evening the first U-boat, Kapitanleutnant Adalbert Schnee's U-201, acknowledged the wireless signals and began the hunt which would result in his torpedoes sinking *Aguila*. So confident was the enemy of the success of Condors and U-boats working together that a surface attack was never considered, although the German armed merchant cruiser *Orion* was actually near the spot and immediately available for action at the time. The *Orion*, known to the Admiralty as Raider 'A', was returning from a foray in the Atlantic camouflaged as a Spanish ship, with a screen of two U-boats. Her movements had not gone entirely unnoticed, as witness an Admiralty signal received by Telegraphist Tom Shuttleworth on watch in HMS *Wallflower's* wireless cabin which read: 'A raider is believed to be in the vicinity of OG71'.

'Well, this is it,' thought Shuttleworth, 'we are not going to survive.' At best, all they could do against such a heavily-armed ship was to attempt to ram. But the threat passed and there were no more signals of that nature, for the Germans ordered *Orion* not to engage the convoy. She continued on her way past Cap Finistère and through the Bay of Biscay to be met by enemy destroyers and escorted in to Bordeaux.

The very successful midnight diversion created by HMS *Bluebell* had drawn five U-boats from the area of the convoy, putting them temporarily off the scent, but after this night's respite spotter planes had soon re-located the convoy next day and from then on the enemy was not to be denied.

What was all too clear, and plaintively echoed in reports of the merchant masters, was that OG71 had been badly in need of more effective air support to deal with the shadowers.

So, long after the wolf pack's triumphant return to Lorient, with the award to U-201's Kapitanleutnant Adalbert Schnee (*Ciscar*, *Aguila*, *Aldergrove*, *Stork*) of his Knight's Cross of the Iron Cross, and to U-564's Oberleutnant Reinhard Suhren (*Empire Oak*, *Clonlara*, *Zinnia*) of the Oak Leaves to his Knight's Cross (for sinking more than 100,000 tons of shipping), the inquest on the unfortunate Gibraltar convoy devolved into smaller, but still important, wrangles, such as why had the corvettes run out of snowflake rockets?

There was the sensible suggestion submitted by corvette *Hydrangea's* captain, following his grimly frustrating attempts to locate oil-covered survivors of *Bath* in the dark, that naval officers and ratings should be issued with whistles and have red lights attached to their lifebelts, as did the merchant seamen, also a loop attached to the lifebelt so that when a man was brought alongside it would be possible to hook him on with a tackle to heave him on board.

And there was a plea by a merchant officer that corvette *Campanula* would have greatly aided rescue work if she had lowered her scrambling nets over the side for exhausted men in the sea to cling on to, instead of relying on heaving lines and her dinghy. A brisk exchange of memos followed, culminating in a sharp signal to *Campanula's* captain — which elicited the dry reply that he had not dropped his scrambling nets for the simple reason that the corvette did not have any, although they had been on order for months.

A rocket went off to the supply officer concerned, with results that may be imagined. Other signals buzzed, including a particularly important one to the Secretary of the Admiralty from C-in-C WA.

> 'Be pleased to inform Their Lordships that it is for consideration that before being accepted in convoy all British, Allied and Neutral vessels should be painted in a dull uniform grey colour, and that no Neutral vessel be accepted in convoy which has any distinctive markings on funnel or hull. The report of interview with the master of ss. *Ciscar* suggests that the two Eire vessels were a definite menace to the safety of the convoy owing to their funnel markings being very conspicuous.'

The Top Secret file of dismal findings on convoy OG71 was passed around the Board of Admiralty for selected staff to digest. The Fourth Sea Lord, on reading the harrowing report by Lieutenant-Commander Cuthbertson, took up his pen to write in the margin the sober observation:

> '*The CO of Zinnia appears to have survived an ordeal which might be described as "awful" with remarkable fortitude.*'

And that was the end of it.

The C-in-C WA directed that a letter be sent to the captain of the ss. *Spero* conveying the Admiralty's warm thanks for his taking over as Commodore ship in trying circumstances and performing that duty well.

The letter was sent, but to the wrong captain.

9
PENNIES FOR THE GIRLS

9

PENNIES FOR THE GIRLS

CAPTAIN Arthur Frith of the lost *Aguila* was stranded for over three weeks in Gibraltar, living in mean conditions in the Victoria Hotel, before being able to gain passage home in another of his company's former Canary cruisers, the ss. *Avoceta*, when she called at the Rock.

The *Avoceta's* captain could only take on four extra passengers from Gibraltar as the ship was already full of refugees; men, women and children, mostly foreign, from Lisbon. Captain Frith and Captain McLean of the sunken *Aldergrove* were among those lucky four.

The *Avoceta*, carrying general stores and mail besides her full complement of passengers, was appointed Commodore ship (Rear-Admiral Greighton) of the homeward-bound convoy HG73, which comprised twenty-five vessels. The convoy had the benefit of an 'air support ship' among its naval escorts, though this was not half as grand as it sounded. HMS *Springbank*, a merchantman converted into a fighter catapult ship, simply carried a single Fairey Fulmar fighter which, once launched, would have to head back for Gibraltar after its mission, having no means of getting back on to its mother ship.

And this was what happened, soon after the convoy set sail from Gibraltar on 17 September. After being catapulted off to harass and chase away a shadowing Focke-Wulf the Fulmar, its guns jammed, flew back home. With its departure the enemy closed in, using again the successful homing-in tactics which had beaten convoy OG71.

Nine ships of the convoy were sunk — plus HMS *Springbank* herself. Among the luckless victims were four of the returning ships of OG71: *Lapwing*, *Empire Stream*, *Cervantes* and *Petrel*.

Five of the vessels were torpedoed on one ghastly night, that of 25 September. And one of those five was *Avoceta*.

It was close to midnight when *Aguila's* sister ship was hit. She sank rapidly, and once again Captain Frith found himself pitched into the dark waters in which his own ship had gone down. Again he was lucky, escaping injury and managing to swim to a raft, from which he was picked up by the corvette HMS *Periwinkle*. He and Captain McLean were among only forty-three survivors from *Avoceta's* large number of passengers and crew — another frightful tragedy.

For the remainder of the voyage home, as he lay for the second time on the deck of a crowded rescuing corvette, Captain Arthur Frith had good reason to ponder on the prophetic last words of the earnest young Wren officer on board *Aguila*:

'... *but you don't need my good wishes — you'll survive.*'

Young Rita Frith was there to greet her father on his arrival at Liverpool.

'He certainly did not bring anything back with him except himself. My mother took me with her to Lime Street Station, Liverpool, to meet him, and I didn't recognise him, he looked so old, more like my grandpa — in fact, now I look back, my grandpa probably looked younger. I remember I was intrigued by the cap Dad wore, it was a khaki forage cap, so he appeared to be half a soldier, half a sailor, the way he was dressed.'

One of Captain Frith's first sombre duties was to journey to London, where, in her cramped headquarters in Great Smith Street, Westminster, he had the painful task of describing the fate of *Aguila* to the Director of the WRNS. Mrs Laughton Mathews would write later:

'I saw the skipper .... he had been torpedoed again on his return journey and was a very shaken man — a little man looking more like a clerk than the hearty seaman. I have never forgotten my talk with him, nor the intense impression he gave me in a few faltering sentences of what it means to go down into the bowels of the sea with the superstructure of the ship on top of you. No doubt he went back into that hell, quietly, unspectacularly, with never a thought that any other course was possible.

'Of the end of *Aguila*, the little slow-moving transport, he used the expression, "It was like potting a sitting bird" . . .'

All the evidence, scant as it was, pointed to the majority of the Wrens being in their cabins, which were on the side of the ship that was hit, when the two torpedoes struck home. It must have resulted in them being killed instantly. The Director, in a personal letter sent to all the relatives after she had seen the captain, emphasised this fact. It was little enough comfort but, she pointed out, at least the girls had been spared any further suffering.

No other information about the convoy, either official or unofficial, was given to anyone, no word on the fate of each ship, which for some questing relatives, ever hopeful that a loved one might still have survived or simply seeking a crumb of consolation in their bereavement, was hard to bear. Some of the treatment meted out to grief-stricken enquirers created bad feeling. There was, for example, the distraught young widow of a crewman of *Aguila*, mother of a baby girl, who called at Yeowards' office and asked to see the captain to find out what had happened to her husband. She was turned away.

It was a distressing time for Yeoman of Signals Fred Buckingham, when he returned home to Liverpool, for he found that the Admiralty had given his address to families of his lost signal staff and some of them called on him, eager that he might give them some comforting words.

In Gibraltar, meanwhile, another of *Aguila's* handful of survivors had further cause to bless his good fortune. Leading Aircraft Mechanic William Churchouse, of the Fleet Air Arm, who had sailed in *Aguila* to join the *Ark Royal* at Gibraltar, duly joined the aircraft carrier, but lost his ship again when she was torpedoed by U-81 off Gibraltar. He then joined HMS *Audacity*, the first of the small 'Woolworth' aircraft carriers, for a passage home — and was plunged into the sea again when she was torpedoed by U-741 off Portugal.

Torpedoed three times in five months. For Churchouse, every day of his life since then has been a bonus.

Captain Frith went back to the war, working for the Ministry of Sea Transport on shore service, then taking part in sea invasion exercises in Scotland and later with the American Forces in similar assault training at Barry, South Wales. He spoke little of the *Aguila* tragedy, even to his family. But the horror and sorrow of it never left him; and, in fact, in the years to come he would be faced by constant reminders of that fateful night.

The news of the death of Chief Wren Madge Barnes had not only stunned her old Sea Ranger crew in Leith, it also affected many others, for local people who had only seen lively young Madge once remembered her; she had just stood out in a crowd as someone different. The alertness and fun in those vivid blue eyes, once seen, was never forgotten.

Immediately after the tragedy there was a call for a fund to be set up in Madge's memory, and the donations started to come in. The Rangers decided to give every £5 subscribed to the purchase of a Sea Rescue Kit, which meant that the money went to give immediate help for those continuing to fight the sea war. Many such kits were sent out during the following months. Additionally, plans were put in hand for a more tangible memorial to Madge, while at this same time, in mid-1942, the first steps were taken towards arranging a memorial to the whole Gibraltar draft.

Canon Ogle of Winchester, father of Second Officer Christine Ogle, leader of the *Aguila* Wrens, wrote asking the other bereaved families if they would care to unite in subscribing to a memorial to the girls. His suggestion met with unanimous approval and the Aguila Wren Memorial Fund was inaugurated with Canon Ogle and Mr Edward Benjamin, father of Chief Wren Cecilly Benjamin, as joint trustees. An account for subscriptions was opened at Barclays Bank, Winchester. A new lifeboat for the RNLI to replace one of those lost at Dunkirk was agreed as the ideal memorial. It would cost £3,700 to build, a considerable sum in those days.

In spite of the reduced circumstances in which many people found themselves in wartime, money towards this target came in from families and friends, large amounts and small, whatever people could afford to give, and every single girl remembered. Every pound, shilling and penny was gratefully acknowledged, including touching contributions by neighbours; a collection in two villages which brought in the munificent sum of £13 10s 9d; pennies from children who gave up their pocket money; and the anonymous person who sold his or her bicycle to realise £3.

But the plan for a memorial lifeboat would have to wait. It was discovered that because of the demands of the fighting forces one could not be built until after the war. In the meantime an interim memorial gift was agreed on the suggestion of the Director of the WRNS.

A new naval escort sloop, almost ready for sea, was to be called HMS *Wren*, as a tribute to the women's Service. It was decided to give some money from the fund to pay for a Sick Bay for the ship, together with stores and fittings. This was done, and a plaque placed in the Sick Bay bearing the following inscription:

> 'In ever-living and loving remembrance of the twenty-two members of the WRNS who gave their lives in the ss. *Aguila*, sunk by enemy action in the morning of 19 August 1941, this Sick Bay is given to HMS *Wren* by their families and friends. "And in the fourth watch of the night Jesus went unto them walking on the sea." St. Matthew XV.25.'

Mrs Laughton Mathews ceremoniously launched the sloop containing this first memorial to the *Aguila* Wrens on a day of September 1942. Coincidentally, only weeks later, time ran out for the U-boat commander who had sunk the ss. *Alva*, Kapitanleutnant Hans Heidtmann, when his U-559 was sunk by a force of British destroyers. Heidtmann survived to be taken prisoner-of-war. He was luckier than Walter Kell, the commander who sank RNN *Bath*. Kell died with his crew when his U-204 was depth-charged and sunk west of Gibraltar.

(The other two 'wolves' who sank ships of OG71, Adalbert Schnee (*Ciscar, Aguila, Aldergrove, Stork*) and Reinhard Suhren (*Empire Oak, Clonlara,* HMS *Zinnia*) both had charmed lives and survived the war.)

In Leith, the permanent memorial to Madge Barnes took shape. The plan was for a plaque to be placed in the parish church of St. Paul's, Leith, the official church of the Guides and Sea Rangers, but Madge's mother emphasised that they were not to spend more than £5 on it, which presented a problem.

They did not want a stone plaque, so the Sea Rangers' skipper, Winifred Shand, went to the Lady Haig factory to see if they could help. They were pleased to do so. A plaque was designed and a copy of it sent to WRNS headquarters for official approval. When Skipper Shand saw the finished work she could not believe how anyone could have made it for the small sum at the Rangers' disposal. It was only later that she discovered that the man who fashioned the plaque had known one of the other Wrens in the *Aguila*, so had done the work in memory of her.

On an emotional day in 1943, the fourth year of war against Hitler tyranny, Madge Barnes' old skipper, now Chief Wren Shand, WRNS, was at St. Paul's for the dedication and unveiling of the plaque before a packed congregation including many young faces who, just like Madge, would soon be off to fight for their country.

10
A Life for Each Life

10

A LIFE FOR EACH LIFE

ON 8 May 1945, the day following VE day, celebrating victory in Europe, Captain Arthur Frith was sent up to Methil, Fife, where the Royal Navy was bringing in surrendered German merchant ships. The German captains and crews were removed under escort, the vessels then being taken over by British crews. The German name of the first ship Captain Frith was given to command was painted out and she was renamed *Empire Lea*. He was to sail her for some time and go on to command other 'Empire' ships operated by the Yeoward Line on behalf of Sea Transport.

Exactly a year later, in May 1946, with the war in the Pacific also over, memories on Merseyside were revived by the sight of the three-masted steamer *Alca*, resplendent in the traditional Yeoward livery, at anchor in the river for the first post-war sailing to Lisbon and the Canary Islands.

Alca was the sole survivor of the Yeoward fleet. Gone were the *Aguila* and *Avoceta*. Gone, too, the *Ardeola*, captured by the Vichy French and torpedoed by the Allies when she was put into operation by the Germans.

Alca had undergone a big refit. As HMS *Alca* she had seen service in Icelandic waters as a depot ship for small craft. Now it was back to the sunshine cruises, and eventually she would be taken over by Captain Frith, whose command she would remain for the next few years.

In the autumn of 1946 Mrs Vera Laughton Mathews said goodbye to the Service which she had managed with such rare accomplishment throughout the war. She stepped down from the WRNS with her dearest wish realised, for this time the Wrens would not be disbanded: it was officially decided to keep the WRNS in being as a permanent peacetime force. She and her girls had done it.

She was made a Dame of the British Empire. And in 1948, at the age of sixty, her autobiography was published (*Blue Tapestry*; Hollis and Carter). By no means the usual sort of personalised life story, it was the combined story of two lives — her own, and that of her beloved Women's Royal Naval Service. Dame Vera had kept few notes and wrote largely from her remarkable memory. The result was a delightfully warm, candid and refreshing book. In it she recalled the *Aguila* incident with the deepest sorrow, remembering poignantly to the hour when the Admiralty's stark message reached her.

'I was in Plymouth in August 1941 when the news came of one of the worst blows our Service suffered. I had been motoring along the south-west coast, inspecting several establishments, and when my mind goes back to the tragic fate of our first draft to Gibraltar, a vivid picture comes of the lovely Cornish hedges heavy with purple veronica, the scent of honeysuckle is still strong and the air still soft in the Devon lanes . . .'

She described her later meeting with *Aguila's* captain but gave no details of the convoy, for she had been given none at the time or afterwards. She was even left with the impression that another officer, not Vice-Admiral Parker, had been its Commodore and had been rescued, for the exact circumstances in which the *Aguila* Wrens had perished remained unexplained, the story of OG71 untold.

Three years later, when a hugely successful novel of the war at sea was published, some of the happenings on OG71 formed the basis for incidents described in its fictional pages, though hardly anyone was aware of the fact except some of those intimately concerned.

Nicholas Monsarrat, from being a raw lieutenant in *Campanula* had gone on to command his own corvette and later, a frigate, but of all his five and a half years spent at sea on Atlantic convoys, OG71 to Gibraltar remained the strongest in his memory.

'That convoy was my worst experience of the war,' he once declared. 'It will live with me for ever.' And it did.

In the pages of *The Cruel Sea* he described the role of the fictional corvette HMS *Compass Rose* in a convoy to Gibraltar which left the bombed city of Liverpool at exactly the same time as did the real convoy OG71 — in 'the smiling weather of late summer' in 1941. He described the early appearance of the first shadowing four-engined Focke-Wulf, circling above them in a sunny sky as the convoy sailed 'on a sea as smooth as old glass', and the gloomy forebodings which the sight of it produced among some men. He described the awesome destruction of a tanker — and the sinking during the night of another ship 'in circumstances of special horror.'

> 'She was known to be carrying about twenty Wrens, the first draft to be sent to Gibraltar: aboard *Compass Rose* they had watched the girls strolling about the deck, had waved to them as they passed, had been glad of their company even at long range. The ship that carried them was the last to be struck that night: she went down so swiftly that the flames which engulfed the whole of her after part hardly had time to take hold before they were quenched . . .'

Monsarrat went on to describe how four of the Wrens were picked up by another ship, only to be finally lost when that vessel too was torpedoed and sank rapidly in the night. Whether this was half-remembered 'fact' or pure fiction, it was of course incorrect; yet, strangely, other naval men who had been on convoy OG71 and who now read *The Cruel Sea* took his account to be true, including the recovery of certain bodies, for such was the paucity of information about the girls and of the convoy itself that even ten years after the event, crews of the various ships still knew only their own part in the affair and often little enough about that.

Monsarrat wrote feelingly of the shadowing aircraft and the 'helpless sense of nakedness' they induced; of the continual sinkings, and the hapless, helpless escorts . . . to anyone who had been there it all rang uncomfortably true; but what really leapt out of the pages as vividly as yesterday was the sudden end of *Compass Rose's* sister corvette, the *Sorrel*. Under a black night sky she was zig-zagging at fourteen knots on a wing of the convoy when suddenly 'a brilliant orange flash split the darkness, flared up again, and then guttered away to nothing'. *Sorrel* sank in less than two minutes. Monsarrat described in emotional terms the extraordinary shock felt by everyone at the dreadful end of their chummy-ship and told how only fifteen survivors were picked up, including her 'reeking, oil-soaked captain' — just as had happened with *Zinnia*.

One of the fifteen survivors of *Zinnia*, Coder Walter Wilkinson, could scarcely believe what he read. He wrote to Monsarrat, who replied confirming that the sinking of *Sorrel* was indeed inspired by the fate of *Zinnia*.

> 'I did not put any actual ships that served in Atlantic convoys,' he wrote, 'but as it happens my ship (*Campanula*) did take part in the Gibraltar convoy in which *Zinnia* was sunk, and I based that chapter on her very sad loss.'

The Cruel Sea went on to cover the whole of the war years of the Battle of the Atlantic, but even at the end of the novel Monsarrat returned to the haunting memory of OG71. In a poignant scene on the very last page of the book, with the war with Germany just ended, the frigate captain and his first lieutenant recall friends and comrades of their corvette days no longer with them. As they talk, the No. 1 recalls: '. . . All those chaps in *Sorrel*. And the Wrens we lost, on that bad Gibraltar convoy.'

Above all, Monsarrat plucked from OG71 his hero for *The Cruel Sea*. For the character of 'Lieutenant-Commander George Ericson, Royal Naval Reserve, formerly of the Far East Line', was firmly based, as far as looks, achievement and reputation were concerned, on none other than HMS *Zinnia's* Lieutenant-Commander Charles George Cuthbertson, RNR. Monsarrat wrote to Cuthbertson to tell him so; they had never lost touch since Cuthbertson's mother had knitted little socks for the novelist's first-born child. At that time, Captain Charles Cuthbertson, DSC, RD, RNR, was in business as a nautical consultant and assessor. He had served with the Navy from the first day of the war to the last, in the latter stages commanding an escort flotilla in the Atlantic, the Far East and the Pacific with great accomplishment. He had then rejoined Union Castle and captained ships of the line before leaving to set up in private practice. Still only in his mid-forties he would shortly begin a new career as a nautical surveyor with the Ministry of Transport.

Cuthbertson remained, in Monsarrat's eyes, the complete master mariner, as faithfully reflected by the quietly resourceful commander in *The Cruel Sea*.

Meanwhile, in these immediate post-war years, the Aguila Wren Memorial Fund had continued. Canon Ogle, its founder, had died, but his place as co-trustee was taken by Mr Edward Bacon, brother of Chief Wren Phyllis Bacon in the doomed draft.

And finally the dream of those who had contributed to the fund in the dark war years was realised. The planned memorial lifeboat for the Royal National Lifeboat Institution was built. Costs had soared nearly four-fold since the idea was first mooted, but the £13,000 now needed was raised by adding to the fund's total of more than £6,000 a legacy to the RNLI by the late Mr James Moorhouse, of St. Anne's-on-Sea, Lancashire.

The date fixed for launching the lifeboat, one of the most modern of its kind, was 28 June 1952, at Aberystwyth. Invitations were sent to every contributor to the fund and a hundred people accepted and travelled the long distance to pay personal tribute. One very special invitation was sent to the former Director of the WRNS, and another to the captain of the *Aguila*.

Captain Arthur Frith, still captaining the *Alca*, had no wish to go to the launching ceremony. There would be so many people, the Press, parents and relatives of the lost Wrens — he felt he could not face it.

For eleven years now he had kept silent about that tragic night when his ship had sunk with the loss of nearly 150 lives, including those unfortunate girls.

How did it feel, as master of the vessel, to be one of only a handful of fortunate survivors? How did he live with the memory of those disastrous ninety seconds and the nightmare burden of appalling casualties? These were questions he never answered. He deliberately avoided all talk of the incident and got extremely upset when anyone tried to draw him out, particularly the newspaper reporters who, he said, 'ask you silly questions'.

But privately he remained haunted by two recurring memories. One was of the Wren officer's parting words on the *Aguila*, a strange conversation that he would repeat many times, word for word, convinced that the girl with a Welsh lilt to her voice had had a presentiment of what was about to happen. His other disturbing memory was of the *Avoceta*. A young girl among the doomed passengers on board that crowded ship had played a record of 'Ave Maria' on the gramophone night and morning. Now he could not bear to hear that song sung. Whenever it was played on the radio he would switch off and walk out of the room; it brought back such painful scenes.

But his employers, Yeowards, practically ordered him to attend the ceremony at Aberystwyth and finally he went along with another Yeoward officer for company.

In brilliant sunshine, thousands of people lined Aberystwyth's decorated promenade that Saturday for the launching of the lifeboat *Aguila Wren*. The service, the speeches, the dedication by the Lord Bishop of St. David's; it was a very moving occasion.

Dame Vera Laughton Mathews who, after a lapse of six years, had specially donned her wartime uniform for the day, told of the background to the launching, recalling the magnificent young women who had set out so excitedly on their pioneer voyage, only to be struck down by the bitterest tragedy. She added with feeling:

> 'To many of those present, this memorial honours the memory of *one* infinitely dear person. Perhaps there is no one in the country who remembers *all* that splendid band as clearly as I do . . .
>
> 'This lifeboat is a beautiful idea for a memorial. And beautiful too is the way the relatives and friends of those young women have persevered through eleven years in raising this fund to their memory. They were a very small band and it was a large sum to raise, but nothing is impossible to love. . . .'

The boat was named by Mrs J.A. Miller, eighty-year-old mother of the late Third Officer Kathleen Miller, of Aberystwyth.

> '. . . . I am proud, and I am sure that mothers of the other twenty-one are proud that *Aguila Wren* will keep fresh the memory of our daughters and their self-sacrifice, and it is not only with pride, but with happiness, that I look forward to her saving the sons and daughters of other mothers from the fate that ours could not escape. . . .'

There were rousing cheers as the lifeboat, manned by Aberystwyth seamen, slid across the promenade and down the beach into the sunlit water.

Mrs Miller afterwards placed the bouquet presented to her on her husband's grave in the local churchyard, where a cross had also been erected to the memory of her daughter lost at sea.

Captain Frith found it all hard to bear. It was distressing talking to the bereaved relatives, perhaps the more so because they were all so kind to him. His ordeal over, he slipped quietly away, avoiding the reporters and photographers.

But the public reminders of the lost Wrens were not over for him yet.

Three years later, in 1955, his long association with the Yeoward Line came to an end when the *Alca* was sold for breaking up.

Yeowards, after losing five vessels in the 1914–18 war, had rebuilt their small fleet, only to lose three more in the war against Hitler. Now, the difficulties of building replacements were too great. *Alca* was the last of the line; the company would build no more ships but continue in charter business with the Canaries.

But, at the age of sixty-five, Captain Frith had not stood on his last bridge. Barely a week after *Alca* went to the breakers he received a call from a ship owner in Copenhagen who wanted to put a couple of his vessels under the British flag. Off to Denmark went the captain to collect his ship and choose his officers. His new command was the motor vessel *Duchy of Normandy*, a cargo ship carrying a dozen or so passengers, and his runs now were over different Atlantic waters, to Canada.

Four years later, in 1959, Dame Vera Laughton Mathews died. She was seventy-one. Since her retirement she had been chairman and then president of the Association of Wrens, so maintaining her long, unique ties with the Service she loved and for which she had done so much. Hers had been a rich life of giving and caring, and winning out against often impossible odds. 'She gained the affection of officers and ratings alike,' said *The Times*. Seldom was there a more profound understatement.

Two years later the former master of the *Aguila* retired at the same age of seventy-one. He would have stayed longer sailing the *Duchy of Normandy*, a very happy ship, running to Canada for apples and other commodities, but the rigours of the North Atlantic in winter made him tired, particularly standing on the bridge in the fog. So he finally ended a career of more than fifty years at sea, retiring to live with his daughter, a nursing sister. Rita Frith:

> 'I suggested Dad stayed at home, which he did. I know he tried to run this bungalow like a ship, and I tried to run it like a hospital, so we compromised and ran it like a hospital ship!'

In retirement the captain became a keen gardener. Certain plants got extra special 'TLC' (tender loving care) from him, all being cherished reminders of Flower-class corvettes. They were wallflowers (after HMS *Wallflower*, which saved him when *Aguila* was sunk); periwinkles (after HMS *Periwinkle* which rescued him after *Avoceta* went down); nigellas (after HMS *Nigella* which saved his son after *his* first torpedoing); pinks (after HMS *Pink* mined off Normandy in the invasion month of June 1944); and Zinnias (after HMS *Zinnia*, blown up on that last disastrous night of OG71).

And still, as the captain tended his garden, the memories of *Aguila* persisted in other places, more than twenty years after she was lost.

In October 1964, the lifeboat *Aguila Wren* was withdrawn from service at Aberystwyth.

In her twelve years there she had been launched twenty-one times, saving fourteen lives. She was now transferred to Redcar, on the Yorkshire east coast, one of the oldest of all the lifeboat stations maintained round the coasts of the British Isles, there to begin a new period of service.

The lifeboat's move coincided with a simple ceremony held at a church in Middlesex.

Mr Edward Benjamin and his wife, the parents of Chief Wren Cecilly Benjamin, had commissioned a memorial to the *Aguila* Wrens to be placed in the parish church of St. Edmund The King, Northwood Hills. The beautiful memorial, twelve feet high and in gold leaf, took the form of the 'Angel of God's Presence' hovering over the sea, with a bronze memorial plaque below. It was consecrated on a Sunday morning in December 1964. The inscription on the plaque read:

'In ever-living and loving remembrance of W/T Chief Wren Cecilly Monica Bruce Benjamin aged 20 and W/T Chief Wren Phyllis Bacon aged 21. Great friends and happy companions who gave their life, their joyous youth, and to duty their loyal devotion. Remembering also the 20 other members of the WRNS and one naval nursing sister who perished with them in the ss. *Aguila*, torpedoed at sea in the morning of 19 August 1941 on their way to take up duties at Gibraltar. "And in the fourth watch of the night Jesus went unto them walking on the sea."'

Throughout the rest of the Sixties and into the Seventies there was a yearly public reminder of the *Aguila* tragedy. It appeared among the In Memoriam notices in *The Times* every 19 August, placed there by the Benjamins, a tribute to their lost daughter and her comrades.

And in 1970, when Nicholas Monsarrat published the second volume of his autobiography, covering his years in the Navy, the *Aguila* incident was remembered again. Monsarrat wrote briefly of some of the harrowing incidents on OG71 — 'that wretched Gibraltar convoy' — though without giving its code name or any details. Unfortunately he mixed up incidents and several of the few 'facts' he did give were wrong, even to recalling how he had personally helped to rescue survivors: 'I was in charge of the scrambling nets aft; it was my pride and privilege to yank from the water half a dozen shipmates of this admired man (Cuthbertson) . . .' Somehow the impression was given that *Campanula* (which at the time had no scrambling nets) had also rescued Cuthbertson himself, when actually the corvette had picked up only two men after steaming past Cuthbertson as he struggled weakly and unseen in the oily sea. But the novelist's mix-ups were excusable for even after all this time no one had a clear picture of the convoy, its true losses and survivors, for the simple reason that no account of it existed; also Monsarrat had served on many other convoys and events had understandably become blurred. But what he did do in his book was to convey in haunting terms the extraordinary depth of feeling that still existed among those who had taken part in the convoy in which the Wrens were lost; the convoy which, he frankly declared in an interview, was his enduring nightmare — 'my worst experience of the war'.

Monsarrat also told in his book how saddened and sickened he had been by the appalling end of HMS *Zinnia*, sunk in seconds, and revealed how, years later, he had based his hero in *The Cruel Sea* on the corvette's plucky captain.

When, shortly after publication of his autobiography, Monsarrat wrote to Cuthbertson for advice on a matter concerning the book, *Zinnia's* captain gently put him right on some of the facts. Monsarrat was suitably contrite. He confessed:

> 'I seem to have made more mistakes than an unmarried mother of twelve! Actually I have confused two different rescue operations, after a lapse of twenty-nine years, and maybe I wrote it the way I wanted to remember it. We will deal with it in any future edition . . .'

On the lighter side, Cuthbertson told Monsarrat how from

time to time in the post-war years he had pulled the leg of *Campanula's* captain by telling him, 'On one occasion you left me to drown!'; to which the dry reply was, 'You did not shout loud enough.'

The following year, on 19 August 1971 — thirty years to the day after the *Aguila* went down — an article appeared in the *Scarborough Evening News* remembering the lost Wrens. Headlined 'Night U-boat wolf-pack killed Scarborough-based Wrens' it recalled the wartime days when the Wrens were a familiar sight in the town and went on to describe as much as was known of the tragic convoy which had claimed twelve of those girls. It was little enough, but was the result of months of diligent correspondence by Mrs Joan Dinwoodie, of Scarborough branch of the Association of Wrens, trying to unearth some of the facts. Even the full names of all the girls had proved hard for her to find.

Though all traces of the Wrens in Scarborough had gone, their one-time Wrenery having since been converted into a block of flats, the memories certainly remained, and a sequel to the article came in the summer of the following year, inspired by a particularly generous donation by the mother of a girl in the doomed draft and added to by contributions from other relatives and friends who had trained with the *Aguila* Wrens. It was the presentation of a memorial seat to the town.

On a warm, sunny Saturday in July 1972 the seat, erected on the Lighthouse Pier, was formally handed over to the town council after a short service of dedication, the plaque on the back of the seat being unveiled to reveal the short inscription: 'In memory of the twelve Scarborough-based members of the WRNS who were lost at sea when the ss. *Aguila* was torpedoed en route to Gibraltar on 19 August 1941. This seat was presented by the relatives and the Scarborough branch of the Association of Wrens to commemorate the thirtieth anniversary of their loss.'

It was a perfect day for the ceremony, with a light breeze rippling the sea and the sharp cries of circling seagulls.

> 'During the prayers, those of us who had known the girls who died seemed very close to them and felt that they would have approved of our gesture. When they were stationed in the town the sands were deserted and the harbour heavily guarded, while we could hear in the distance the laughter of

children on the beach and the chugging of engines as the holiday cruising boats approached the pier. The contrast between those wartime days and the happy atmosphere of the holiday season seemed to emphasise the reason for their sacrifice.

'There must be many ex-Wrens visiting Scarborough and we hope that they will make a point of walking to the end of the Lighthouse Pier to rest on our seat to enjoy the view across the South Bay, and perhaps remember their own far-off Navy days and those of their Service who did not come back.'

A few months later the lifeboat *Aguila Wren*, stationed on the same coast farther north, came to the end of her life with the RNLI. In her eight years at Redcar she had been called out fifty-three times and saved twenty-four lives. Altogether, since her launching at Aberystwyth in 1952, she had been called out seventy-four times and saved a total of thirty-eight lives, nearly twice as many souls as the girls whose memory she perpetuated.

Normally, when a lifeboat came to the end of its active life, it was sold off to the highest bidder on condition that it lost its identity, and usually finished its days as an inshore fishing boat. But it was felt that the *Aguila Wren* deserved a better fate, that it was only right that the memorial to the lost Wrens should be kept alive, the boat retaining its name.

So the RNLI looked around for a new home for it and found that the Sea Cadets at Scunthorpe, Lincolnshire, were keen to have the boat. It seemed the ideal home for it, fitting that it should go on to be used for training young men in seamanship while keeping its gallant name and memories.

Everything was arranged for the boat to be handed over to the Sea Cadets on a Sunday morning in May 1973.

When a letter from Yeoward Brothers inviting him to the ceremony dropped on to Captain Frith's doormat at his bungalow in Wirral he was extremely reluctant to go. It was twenty years since he had attended the launching of *Aguila Wren* but the memory of that ordeal remained with him. He was now eighty-three years old, still active and independent, never missing the Battle of the Atlantic service in Liverpool each May, but this occasion was especially hard for him to face. However, after a lot of persuasion from his daughter, and pressure from his son and daughter-in-law, he agreed to go.

The ceremony at Keadby Lock was an impressive one attended by local dignitaries, RNLI and Sea Cadets officials, together with a director of Yeowards and visitors including relatives of some of the lost girls. As the boat was blessed by the Sea Cadets chaplain and the ensign hoisted, memories of the ship after which she was named came flooding back for the master who had survived, and who to his final embarrassment was pressed by one of the relatives into having his photograph taken with her.

Then it was over, and Captain Frith returned to retirement.

He lived on for five more years, happy to see his grandchildren married, taking longer to get ready for the ceremonies than the brides; proud, later, to hold in his arms his two great-grandchildren, a girl and a boy, whom he hoped would grow up to be a sailor; and never forgetting the words of the Wren officer on board the *Aguila* hours before the ship sank . . . 'But this is goodbye for me, and I wish you all the luck in the world, but you don't need my good wishes — *you'll survive.*' He would still repeat that conversation over and over, maintaining till the day he died that she had a presentiment of what was about to happen. And how true she had been about his own long, full life.

Captain Arthur Frith died peacefully on 5 January 1979, four days after being photographed with his great-grandchildren. His daughter:

> 'Dad had a large scar on his back. I did not know that until just before he died, when he was confined to bed for the last two days. When I asked him how he got it, he just laughed and said, "Something struck me on the back when the *Aguila* sank." I said, "What was it?" He replied, "I don't know, but it felt like a German pocket battleship." And he said no more.'

The names of those who had no grave but the sea were commemorated on official naval war memorials, but relatives of the *Aguila* Wrens seeking to visit the appropriate memorial were surprised and disappointed to find that the girls were not listed together but were split up to appear on different memorials at three manning ports: Portsmouth, Chatham and Plymouth.

Enquiries to the War Graves Commission as to why the girls who had died together should be separated in this way to appear on memorials at ports with which they had no connection, brought the reply that the Commission had simply followed Admiralty instructions. It was a regrettable case of wires getting crossed; one more sadness occasioned by the continued lack of official information about the *Aguila* incident.

The girls, however, are entered in the beautiful calf-skin vellum pages of the WRNS Book of Remembrance, which lists the names of more than 300 officers and ratings who died, from many causes, at home and overseas, while serving with the Wrens. The book is lodged in the church of St. Mary-le-Strand, London, the official church of the WRNS.

Meanwhile, up in Scotland every year, in the parish church of St. Paul's, Leith, a wreath is laid at the plaque to Madge Barnes by the Kirk Session.

Little Madge and the others of her pioneer band are not forgotten. They live on as they died, ever young.

The Memory

THE Medical Officer of HMS *Leith* writing from Canada: 'So many times these past forty years have I thought of those brave girls who gave their young lives for Britain and the Empire. Each year, at the Cenotaph service, when the chaplains remind us of those who made the supreme sacrifice, I think of those Wrens and I get a lump in my throat. I remember one time our eldest daughter was with me and observed me weeping as the Bishop spoke. She couldn't understand why I wept nor could I make her understand. I could see those girls, could see that ship, could re-live the horror and anguish of that nightmare.'

THE *AGUILA* WRENS

Second Officer
Christine Emma Ogle

Third Officers:
Cecelia Mary Blake Forster
Margaret Eulalie Chappé Hall
Isabel Mary Milne Holme
Cecilia Alex Bruce Joy
Victoria Constance McLaren
Florence Macpherson
Kathleen Miller
Josephine Caldwell Reith

Chief Wrens:
Phyllis Bacon
Margaret Watmore Barnes
Cecilly Monica Bruce Benjamin
Dorothy Bonsor
Madeleine Gladys Cooper
Mary Grant
Mildred Georgina Norman
Elsie Elizabeth Shepherd
Catherine Johnston Slaven
Beatrix Mabel Smith
Ellen Jessie Waters
Rosalie Wells

Nursing-Sister
Kate Ellen Gribble, QARNNS

ACKNOWLEDGEMENTS

NIGHTMARE CONVOY is the result of three years' research which, at times, it would have been impossible to continue but for the help of a number of people who, like the authors, were determined to see the story of the *Aguila* Wrens told at last. We are grateful to them all for information and photographs.

Apart from those mentioned in the book our special thanks are due to Rita Frith, Anne Wills, Winifred A. Shand, Anne Watson, Claire M. Rees and Eileen Duce.

We also acknowledge the assistance of the Royal Norwegian Embassy, Association of Wrens, Flower Class Corvette Association and Royal National Lifeboat Institution.

We are indebted to all those we could trace who lived the convoy, and in particular to Captain C.G. Cuthbertson, DSC, RD, RNR and Captain H.G. Chesterman, MBE, DSC, RD, RNR.